Hopeful Compositions

Sermons from Partway Up the Mountain

Steve Elderbrock

Parson's Porch Books
www.parsonsporchbooks.com

Hopeful Compositions: Sermons from Partway Up the Mountain
ISBN: Softcover 978-1-949888-92-8
Copyright © 2019 by Steve Elderbrock

All rights reserved. No part of this book may be reproduced or transmitted in any form or by any means, electronic or mechanical, including photocopying, recording, or by any information storage and retrieval system, without permission in writing from the publisher.

To:

G. Terry Bard,
who got this whole "pastor" thing started
and
to my parents,
William and Virginia Elderbrock,
who got pretty much everything else in my life started

Contents

Sermons Matter 7
Preface 9

I. The Basics

The Raciest Sermon I've Ever Preached 13
Song of Songs 8:6-7; Psalm 139:1-6, 26
4-D Love 17
Ephesians 3:14-21
Living Unconditionally, Not Transactionally 21
Psalm 37:1-11, 39-40; Luke 6:27-38
Faces & Stomachs & Bodies (Oh My!) 25
Psalm 27; Philippians 3:17 – 4:1
The Something That Changes Everything 28
1 Kings 19:1-15a
For Freedom 33
Galatians 5:1, 13-25
A Commandment Very Close to Us 40
Luke 10:25-37; Deuteronomy 30:9-14

II. Snapshots from the Church Year

Good Old Zephaniah 49
Zephaniah 3:14-20
I've Looked at Clouds From Both Sides Now 53
Psalm 99; Luke 9:28-36
All in the Family 57
Joel 2:12-17; Romans 10:8b-13
Our Heavenly Gardener 60
Psalm 63:1-8; Luke 13:1-9
The Spirit of Understanding 64
Romans 8:12-17; Acts 2:1-21

III. Outside the Lectionary, Inside an Election

That Other Creation Story 69
Genesis 2:4b-25
Keeping Our Brothers and Sisters 76
Genesis 3:22 – 4:16, 25-26
Could We Find Ten? 83
Genesis 18:16-33; Ezekiel 16:48-50
Don't Look Back 88
Genesis 19:1-3, 12-26; Luke 9:57-62
Seeing the Face of God 94
Genesis 32:3-21, 33:1-11
On the Cusp of God's Promise 99
Numbers 13:25 – 14:45
Unexpected Allies 104
Joshua 2:1-24
Lessons from Jericho 109
Joshua 6:1-27
God's Chosen 113
Isaiah 45:1-25
Fire Escape 116
Daniel 3:1-30
Writing on the Wall 122
Daniel 5:1-31
Praying at Open Windows 128
Daniel 6:1-28
A Whale of a Story 132
Jonah 1:1-17, 2:1-10

Sermons Matter

Parson's Porch Books is delighted to present to you this series called Sermons Matter.

We believe that many of the best writers are pastors who take the role of preacher seriously. Week in, and week out, they exegete scripture, research material, write and deliver sermons in the context of the life of their particular congregation in their given community.

We further believe that sermons are extensions of Holy Scripture which need to be published beyond the manuscripts which are written for delivery each Sunday. Books serve as a vehicle for the sermon to continue to proclaim the Good News of the Morning to a broader audience.

We celebrate the wonderful occasion of the preaching event in Christian worship when the Pastor speaks, the People listen and the Work of the Church proceeds.

Take, Read, and Heed.

David Russell Tullock, M.Div., D.Min.
Publisher
Parson's Porch Books

Preface

Just about every single day since being ordained as a pastor, I have felt like Admiral James Stockdale at the 1992 Vice-Presidential debate, when he said: "Who am I? What am I doing here?"

Being a pastor was never on my radar. I grew up, or at least was born and raised, in Findlay, Ohio, and my family attended a wonderful congregation there: First Presbyterian Church. It was in this congregation, and literally in their beautiful sanctuary, that I was baptized, confirmed, and, eventually, ordained. It is the only congregation that I have ever officially been a member of, and I will always consider it "home." The two pastors during my entire childhood and teen years were Terry Bard and Dean Carzoo. Theirs were the only sermons I heard for the first 18 years of my life, and they set the bar high for me.

I graduated from Denison University with degrees in Philosophy and Cinema, and then wandered for a few years through Yale University (trying my hand at Philosophy) and Hollywood, California (trying my hand at Cinema) before returning to Ohio, to Bowling Green State University, where I obtained a M.A. in American History. I fully intended to go on and earn a Ph.D., but God had other plans. While in Bowling Green, I reconnected with First Presbyterian Church of Findlay and with Terry Bard, who one day suggested I consider going to seminary. It was, and remains, one of the most outlandish suggestions I've ever heard. Yet I was unable to shake it, and when I finally realized, with some help from Saint Augustine, that this might be more than a mere suggestion and the true source might be from higher up than my childhood pastor, I returned to Terry Bard's office to ask: "Now what?" Another question I have been asking ever since.

I graduated from the Candler School of Theology at Emory University, and was ordained by the Presbyterian Church (USA) in 1997.

I was blessed to begin figuring out what it really meant to "be" a pastor and a preacher in the loving care of the First Presbyterian Church in LeRoy, Minnesota, my own personal version of Lake Wobegon. The people there welcomed me with open arms, put up with all my early mistakes, and lovingly sent me on my way when I felt the Spirit calling me elsewhere. That elsewhere was Ottawa, Ohio, and then, in 2013, Burnsville, North Carolina.

This book is dedicated to my friends in Findlay, Leroy, Ottawa, Burnsville, and all points in between, and to everyone who has guided me, challenged me, and/or comforted me along this 22+ year journey I never had any idea I'd be taking.

And thanks to you for reading.

Steve Elderbrock

I. The Basics

The Raciest Sermon I've Ever Preached
Song of Songs 8:6-7; Psalm 139:1-6, 26

August 14, 2016

The Song of Songs is, to say the least, a fascinating book of the Bible. Essentially a dialogue between two lovers, there are a few comments thrown in by others along the way. It's one of those books that, as you read it, makes you wonder how it ever ended up in the Bible. It is, well, let's just say it: kind of a racy book. I distinctly remember stumbling onto the Song of Songs in my early teen years when I was attempting to read the entire Bible front to back; I had made that long slog through Leviticus and Numbers and Deuteronomy, through all those Kings and Chronicles which even as a history buff I couldn't keep track of, and then the Psalms, well, the short ones weren't too bad, but they ARE poetry, and, I mean, c'mon, will I ever get through all this boring Old Testament stuff? Then I got to the Song of Songs and I started coming across references to "breasts," and other such body parts and, well, that was kind of intriguing and exciting at that age: "What the heck? This is in the Bible? God knows about breasts? Does the pastor know this is in here?" I was amazed to discover the Bible included a slightly erotic, sensual, no-holds-barred love poem. One that expresses the richness of love between two people, that deep, passionate, committed love that not only draws people together but keeps them together for a lifetime.

But the question remains: "Why is this book in the Bible? Does the Bible need a sensual, passionate love poem?" Although to our modern sensibilities this book might seem strange, at least unusual compared to other books in the Bible, many ancient Christian writers and preachers embraced this book. St. Bernard of Clairvaux, for example, preached 86 sermons on just the first 35 verses of this book. I'm going to limit myself to one, at least for the moment.

This book has been interpreted as revealing not just the love of two human beings for each other, but the love between God and us and the love between Christ and Christ's Church, between Christ and you and me. Read in those ways, the Song of Songs really gets fascinating. To think about this kind of love, this deep, passionate, intimate, sensual, physical love between God and us, well, that really is intriguing, isn't it? That'll really get your blood pumping, even more than those references to "breasts did as a teenager. Is that how God loves us, like the lovers in this love poem, and is that how we are to love God in return?

Too many of us Christians were brought up to believe that whenever the love of God was mentioned there always had to be judgment with it as a counterweight. Sure God loves us, but in a stern, solemn way, often with God wagging God's finger at us. Sure God loves you, but you'd better be good. Sure God loves you, but in a way reminiscent of your high school principal, ready to call you down to his office at the first sign of trouble. Now imagine God loving us in the way the Song of Songs describes it, deeply, passionately; imagine God saying "I've set you as a seal on my heart" and "my love for you is greater than death, it is a flame that can never be quenched." God begins to sound like a love-sick teenager who has just taken her first poetry class.

Of course that idea – not God as a teenager but God loving us passionately – is nothing new. There were people in the early history of the Christian Church who took this idea literally, particularly women in some places in the early Church. There were women who, instead of marrying another human being, would devote their lives to Christ, to the point where there would even be wedding ceremonies performed acknowledging this commitment to Christ rather than a human husband, sometimes with rings and all the trappings. There are certain writers in the early Church - Hildegard of Bingen, Julian of Norwich, Mechthild of Magdeburg (who has one of the best names in the entire history of the early Church) and others - who write incredibly intimate and passionate, but highly spiritual accounts of their personal relationship with Christ.

We're talking about love in the richest sense of that word, a word we here in the modern world have unfortunately drained of much of its richness and depth by using it so often and so cavalierly. We talk about how we love ice cream, we love chocolate, "I love your new dress," "I love this new TV show," we use it as a slightly more intense form of "like," and thus we render it so shallow a word most of the time. But The Song of Songs reminds us of the true meaning of "love," of the intensity and passion of hearts calling to each other across space and time, of a longing and a desire that goes so much deeper than our feelings about ice cream or chocolate.

And then there are all the references to bodies, the love of bodies. Have you ever thought about how much God loves your physical body? God did create it, after all. But so many of us have grown up being told that the body, physical flesh, is bad, even evil. But Song of Songs reminds us that God made our bodies, and that God loves our bodies, not just as a Creator but as a lover. God sees you not the way we often see ourselves, as needing to lose a few pounds or get rid of those wrinkles; God looks at you and says: "Ah, those eyes, that face, those breasts – your eyes are doves, your cheeks, wrinkles and all, are like halves of a pomegranate, your breasts are like two fawns that feed among the lilies." Can you believe that God loves you that way - not just your soul, but your body? That is the depth and the fervor of God's love for each one of us. This is pretty radical stuff, folks. I'm a little surprised some of our Puritan ancestors in the faith haven't risen from their graves to turn off my microphone yet.

But this is important, this reminder that we are God's beloved and that God's faithful love never ends. God's passionate, intimate, authentic love for us never ends. It is also important to be reminded that anytime we love another human being in this God-like way, through family, through marriage, through friendship, we are reflecting and embodying the way God feels about us. God IS love. Not just some abstract appreciation for things or people, but real, deep, even physical, love, the kind that writer Brian Doyle describes as: "extraordinary ordinary succinct ancient naked stunning perfect simple ferocious love."

I know, this all sounds pretty racy for some of us Presbyterians to even be thinking about, much less talking about. But this is the way God loves each and every one of us, his creation, his human lovers. This also gives a new perspective to some of the references in the Old Testament which allude to God being jealous, those passages that even refer to God as feeling like a jilted lover, who has reached out to us with a passionate embrace of love and been rebuffed, ignored. We have turned away and gone after other "loves" instead – idols - things or people or institutions that do not and cannot love us the way God does. Have you ever considered that God loves you so much that God gets a little upset when you turn away from God, not so much because God is jealous, but because God knows that you are sacrificing real love, God's love, for a pale reflection, for a love that cannot truly satisfy you? God gets upset when we turn away because God knows the kind of love that we are cutting ourselves off from.

I invite you in the coming week to ponder and reflect on all this, not so much up here in your head, but deeper down in your heart. Maybe do a little reading on your own in the Song of Songs, maybe in bed under the covers with a flashlight after everyone else is asleep. Know and believe that God loves you this way. But then begin to ponder how we can begin to show that sort of love to God, and to all the others who God loves just as much as us.

May you have a good, and interesting, and passionate week!

Amen.

4-D Love
Ephesians 3:14-21

July 29, 2018

Today's reading is actually a prayer, one of a number of prayers that Paul offers to and for the Ephesians in this letter and also, across the ages, to and for us. His prayer is that we might have the ability to understand and grasp the power of love.

I would argue that love is the greatest power and the strongest force in the universe. Although it is easy to forget that, especially here in the modern world. We live in a world in which so many other things give the appearance and illusion of greater power than love. What good is love against an army or a gun or a nuclear bomb? Too often hatred and fear and violence seem more powerful than love, which seems to get trampled in the dust. To say that love is the greatest power and strongest force in the universe can sound wildly naïve because so often we think of love as something relatively weak, passive, ineffective. How can love stand against all these other forces that seem to dominate and overpower our world today?

So let me pose another question: who is the most powerful Being in the universe? I hope you might consider "God" to be the best answer to that question. God, who created everything in the universe including the universe itself. God, who holds everything together. God, who, presumably, could destroy the entire universe, if God desired. So if God is the most powerful Being in the universe, let me also remind you what John writes a number of times in his letters: "God is love."

Logic tells us that if A = B, and A = C, then B = C. This is called the Transitive Property of Equality. If God is the Most Powerful Being in the Universe and God is Love, then the Most Powerful Being, the Most Powerful Force, in the Universe is Love.

I think this is the direction in which Paul is heading in today's passage, although he doesn't specifically say that. What Paul does say is: "I pray that you will have the power to grasp the width and the length and the height and the depth of love." Did you realize that love is four-dimensional? Paul is saying something here akin to "love is the most powerful force in the universe."

Commentators and scholars over the years have argued about what Paul is talking about here. Some, for example, claim that by the "height" of love Paul means the angels, and by the "depth" of love Paul means the demons and by "length" and "width" Paul means everything in between. Maybe.

Here's how I explain what Paul is saying:

The "width" of Love: "Width" is about "broadness" and "extension." How wide and broad is love? I have heard it suggested that when Jesus opened his arms there on the cross, he was opening his arms wide, to embrace the whole of creation. God's love is extended to all and for all, and not just all human beings, but all of creation, all creatures. In other words, God's love is so wide that it is limitless. There is no limit to the wideness of God's love. Or as our first hymn put it: "Jesus, Thy boundless love to me no thought can reach, no tongue declares."

The "length" of Love: When I think about length I often think of time. "How long is the sermon going to be this morning?" "How long is this meeting going to last?" "How long is this meeting going to seem to last?" (the answer to those last two questions is often quite different) We often talk about length, beyond the physical, in terms of time. So in those terms, how long does love last? Scripture declares again and again about God's love that it is "never-ending." God's love is eternal, timeless. How long is love? Forever. And I think that is one way we can distinguish between the rather shallow way that we often talk about love and true, authentic, Godly love. We sometimes talk about falling in and out of love. But love in the Godly sense cannot be fallen in and out of, it is eternal. Limitless.

The "height" of Love: You can never rise so high in this world, you can never be so successful, so rich, so powerful, that you don't still desire love. I don't want to spoil the ending for anyone who has never seen it, but just watch what may be the greatest movie ever made: *Citizen Kane*, all about Charles Foster's Kane's lifelong desire to recapture lost love. His money, his fame, his power can't fill that emptiness. No one ever rises so high that they rise about the need for, the desire for, love.

And in terms of **the "depths" of love**, you can never sink so low, into pits of despair or darkness or failure or hopelessness, that God's love can't reach down and grab hold of you, even into the depths of Hell itself. No one is ever beyond saving by God.

What I think Paul is really saying when he says: "I want you to grasp the width and the length and the height and the depth of love," is that love really has no dimensions. There are no limits to love, not in any way, shape, or form. You can't put love in a box, any more than you can put God in a box, although God knows many people keep trying.

This is why I am confident in asserting that love is the greatest force, the strongest power, in the universe. Everything else is limited, finite. Even armies and guns and nuclear bombs. They will all rust and wear out and turn to dust, as will we and our entire human civilization, someday. Everything in this world will pass away but love never ends. Paul himself will assert this to the Corinthians.

The greatest power in the universe is love…and God gives it to us. At the end of this passage in Ephesians, Paul reminds us that God's power working through us, the power of love, can accomplish things we can't even imagine. How do we address all the problems in our world, in our country? How do we address violence and war, immigration, poverty, division, hatred? I don't know the details, but all the solutions must start and end with love.

Oh, that sounds so weak, so naïve. But it isn't. Love is the only power that can address all our human problems, in a lasting, long-term, win-win way.

I am more and more convinced that the greatest gift we Christians can give the world is to show and share the power of love. Notice that Paul says the power of love is the "fullness of God." God is full of love, and God wants to fill our world full of love, through us. Each and every one of us. That requires us, first, to fill ourselves with love – love for God, love for our neighbors, love for ourselves. That's where this love thing starts to get difficult and complicated. But I would suggest to you that our primary task as followers of Christ is to fill ourselves, our let ourselves be filled, every day, with God's love so that as we go out our world that love overflows out of us. Let's go and fill our world with love, as opposed to all the other stuff our world seems so full of these days.

Amen.

Living Unconditionally, Not Transactionally
Psalm 37:1-11, 39-40; Luke 6:27-38

February 24, 2019

If anyone ever asks you to sum up in seven words the message of the Bible, or the essence of what it means to be a follower of Jesus Christ, you could do a lot worse than this verse from Psalm 37: "Trust in the Lord and do good."

That pretty much sums it up: "Trust in the Lord and do good." It is a great summary of the essence of Christianity, and yet admittedly it is also a little vague. Not so much the first part about trusting in the Lord – that's pretty clear. But the "do good" part, that leaves a lot of room for interpretation. I'll bet if I started throwing out examples from daily life, we might have some disagreement amongst ourselves about what is good or not so good in any particular instance. "Do good" is a great general statement, but we might have difficulty applying it to the circumstances and situations of daily life.

That's where Luke 6:27-38 comes in. In this passage, I see Jesus attempting to fill in some of the gaps and offer some details about what it means to "do good". So what does it mean to do good, according to Jesus?

"Love your enemies. Do good to those who hate you. Bless those who curse you. Pray for those who mistreat you." Turn the other cheek, give you shirt as well as your coat, don't judge, don't condemn, forgive, and give expecting nothing in return.

Yikes. No wonder Jesus prefaces all this with: "I say this to you who are willing to hear…" As one commentator on this passage remarked, congregations generally respond to this passage with about as much enthusiasm as his kids respond to spinach on the dinner table. This is tough message to swallow, a pretty tall order, difficult to hear and even more difficult to do.

And much of that has to do with the fact that what Jesus is telling us is that doing good is not transactional. Doing good is not a quid pro quo, it is not "you scratch my back and I'll scratch yours." It is not "an eye for an eye and a tooth for a tooth," which, as a wise man once reminded us, just leaves everyone blind and unable to chew their food.

That's transactional, and we humans, and I fear we modern-day Americans, are becoming more and more transactional: "We will be good to your country if you are good to us. We will allow you to come live in our country only if you can do something to help us, if you have the right skills." I fear we modern-day Christians also think of things too often in transactional terms: "If you are good to me, I will be good to you. If you forgive me, I will forgive you. If you pray for me, I will pray for you. I will treat you the way you treat me." So we have even turned the Golden Rule into a transaction. The Golden Rule says: "Do unto others as you would have them do unto you," or as Jesus says it in Luke 6: "Treat people in the same way that you want them to treat you." But we too often turn that into "Do unto others as they do unto you, treat others the way they treat you." That is not God's idea of "doing good." God's idea is not about how people actually treat you, not what they actually do to you, but how you want to be treated, what you wish they would do. It is aspirational and inspirational, not transactional. Indeed one of the problems with treating everything as transactional is that it reduces all behavior to the lowest common denominator.

Transactional behavior is not inspirational at all. That's what Jesus means when he says that if you just do good to those who do good to you, or only forgive those who forgive you, or give knowing you will be repaid, it is not really commendable. Anyone can do that. Most people do. But Jesus wants us to do better and to be better than others. Jesus wants those who follow him to aspire to something higher and nobler than quid pro quo. Give. Bless. Pray. Forgive. Not expecting anything in return or any result, regardless of the result, or the reaction of the other person. Do it because that's how God wants you to behave.

I'm reminded of a story about the poet Mary Oliver. She was once asked by someone what the purpose of beauty is. And she replied that the purpose of beauty is "to make us ache to be worthy of it." I think that is akin to what Jesus is saying about being good – we ache to be good so that we can be worthy of our God who is Good.

So then, why love? Not in order to be loved but in order to be LOVING. Why forgive? Not in order to be forgiven but in order to be FORGIVING. Why pray? Not in order to be prayed for, but in order to be PRAYING. Why bless? Not in order to be blessed, but in order to be a BLESSING. Our actions and behavior, our doing good, have nothing to do with how other people respond. This is not transactional at all. We are to do good because our God is Good and God wants us to do good, and we want to be more and more the people God wants us to be.

Of course we are not there yet. I fear our society and many of us are nowhere near getting away from transactional thinking, from viewing the world from that perspective. I am reminded of some wisdom I read recently from another poet, Maya Angelou: *'I'm working at trying to be a Christian and that's serious business. It's not something where you think, 'Oh, I've got it done. I did it all day—hot diggety.' The truth is, all day long you try to do it, try to be it. And then in the evening, if you're honest and have a little courage, you look at yourself and say, 'Hmmm. I only blew it 86 times. Not bad.'*

I'm trying to be a Christian." She went on to say: *"'I'm always amazed when [people] walk up to me and say, 'I'm a Christian.' I always think, 'Already? You've already got it? My goodness, you're fast.'"*

We are called to shining lights to the world, to let our light shine before others, to be beacons of hope, to be examples and models for the world of how to live with love and goodness and blessing and prayer and hope; unconditionally, not transactionally. So let your light shine, don't hide it under a bushel basket of transactional thinking. Let it shine.

I believe that is our task and our calling as individuals, as a congregation, as followers of Christ. I think God is telling us it is time to stop thinking about life in transaction al terms, to show the world how to do that. To love and do good and be good, simply because that is who God wants us to be. And maybe that starts with us, right now, here today.

Amen.

Faces & Stomachs & Bodies (Oh My!)
Psalm 27; Philippians 3:17 – 4:1

March 17, 2019

This week I was struck by all the bodily imagery in our two Scripture readings. Did you notice the references to head and heart and faces and stomachs? References to our bodies and Jesus's body and even, strangely, God's body. Let's start with the reference to God's body in Psalm 27: "Come, my heart says, seek God's face. Lord, I do seek your face." I've been reflecting all week on what it means to seek God's face. What it means for God to even have a face. It implies, doesn't it, that God might have a physical body.

We are told at the end of the Book of Deuteronomy that Moses was unique among prophets, and presumably human beings, in that he talked to God "face to face" and yet earlier there is a story of Moses asking if he can see God's face and God tells him that no one can see God's face and live, so God merely let's Moses see God's backside as God passes by. So can we, mere humans, see God's face, and what would it mean if we could?

In thinking about God's face, I began considering the importance of a face generally. Our face is the part of us that is the most unique and recognizable. Have you ever been in the grocery store or the post office and you were sure you saw someone you knew from the back? You go up and start talking to them, "Hi Judy, good to see you!" and she turns around and it isn't Judy at all, in fact her face doesn't look a thing like Judy's. Our faces are the most recognizable parts of our bodies. Scientists and computer programmers are working overtime on facial recognition technology so that even computers will be able to recognize us. How? By our faces.

So maybe when Psalm 27 tells us to seek God's face, it is telling us to try to recognize God's presence in our world, here and now, in "the land of the living," in this earthly life, even in and among our own human bodies and faces. Because we are told, after all, that we humans are made in the image of God, so perhaps God's face can be seen even in other human beings. Or as Fred Rogers so famously reminded us in the wake of tragic events, "look for the helpers."

And perhaps this idea of looking for God's face is also a reminder that our Christian faith is not just about abstract spiritual ideas but about addressing the needs of real human bodies. Maybe seeking God's face means to be aware of the physical needs of other human beings. As Jesus always taught: feed the hungry, give a drink to those who are thirsty, visit those real human bodies who are in prison, and welcome the very real physical bodies of the refugees and the immigrants.

Yet Paul, in writing to the Philippians, reminds us not to get TOO caught up in the body, the earthly, physical body. Too many people, Paul writes, live "as enemies of the cross," they focus too much on their bodies, they make their stomachs their god, they focus on earthly things. Paul's message is to not make our bodies an idol, a god. I fear that is too much the case in our modern world, when we are so concerned with how we look, with how we appear on social media, with millions spent on cosmetic surgeries and diet plans. We get so focused on such things.

But Jesus modelled for us how to balance a necessary concern for the physical with an even more necessary concern for the spiritual. After all, Jesus often ate dinner with others, and told his disciples to feed the hungry, and his first recorded miracle was turning water into wine at a wedding feast, and yet Jesus also posed the question: "Isn't life more than food, and the body more than clothes?" Jesus knew he was more than just a human body, even on the cross. Jesus was more than just his human body, and so are we. And, as Paul reminds us, Jesus came to save us from ourselves and to transform our humble bodies.

It is on the cross, and in his resurrection, that Jesus truly transforms us, both in body and spirit. For it was in those moments that Jesus himself was transformed, as well. He suffered, horribly, in body and in spirit there on the cross. When he was resurrected it was therefore not just in spirit but in body as well. That's why he told Thomas to touch his hands and his feet, and that's why some of the gospel accounts of the resurrected Lord describe how he ate food, to prove he wasn't a ghost. He was resurrected in body, transformed in body.

And so it is with us today. We are, transformed, together, as the body of Christ. The human body of Jesus Christ transformed into a community, many bodies taking care of others, both in body and in spirit. Seeking to be the hands and the feet, the eyes and the ears and even the heart of Christ. And perhaps even the face of Christ, the face of God. And so we have come full circle, back to seeking God's face. Except now, as a community of faith, we are not just seeking God's face, we are being God's face, being the physical body of Christ and face of God for all the world to see.

Amen.

The Something That Changes Everything
1 Kings 19:1-15a

June 23, 2019

Before jumping into today's passage, it is worth remembering what has happened to Elijah just before this passage.

The once united kingdom of David was at this moment sharply divided, with the kingdom of Israel in the north and the kingdom of Judah in the south. A man named Ahab was the king of Israel, and the main thing Scripture says about Ahab was that "he was a worse king than any king that had come before him" at least in God's eyes. Among other things, Ahab had reinstituted the worship of the pagan god Baal, largely at the request of his even more infamous wife, Jezebel. Against them both stood the prophet Elijah, proclaiming the one, true God.

In chapter 18 of 1 Kings, Elijah is so confident of God's power that he proposes a contest with Ahab – Elijah himself alone against all the prophets of Baal. Whoever can call down fire from their god wins. The prophets of Baal go first, and they go through all the motions – they weep, they wail, they cry out they plead with Baal, they even cut themselves to use the blood as a sacrifice. Nothing happens. At one point Elijah is so confident he taunts them: "Maybe your god is just asleep or has wandered away." When Elijah's turn comes, he is again so confident that he not only has the people pour water on the altar and the wood three times, until it is water-logged, he also has them dig a trench around the altar and fill it with water. Then Elijah quietly prays to God, and immediately fire comes down from heaven and burns up the water-logged wood and altar and even dries up all the water in the trench. Supremely confident, Elijah has the prophets of Baal put to death, all 400 of them. As a coda, when Ahab heads home in his chariot, Elijah, on foot and full of God's Spirit, runs and beats him back to Jezreel. Elijah is riding high.

Which is what makes the beginning of today's story so odd. Jezebel, having heard of what Elijah did, sends him a message: "May my gods strike me down if by tomorrow I haven't done to you what you did to Baal's prophets." This is the 9th century B.C. version of waking up with a severed horse head in your bed. It terrifies Elijah. After all the success he has just had, he suddenly fears for his life and flees. I don't know exactly why, but I don't think Elijah has lost faith in God, I think he has lost faith in himself. Perhaps he thinks he overstepped somehow, went too far. This happens sometimes to people of faith. You may remember stories about Mother Teresa, for example. After her death it was revealed that she often had deep doubts about the work she was doing, which sounds amazing to those of us who looked to her as almost a saint, but it happens. This is perhaps akin to what St. John of the Cross famously called "the dark night of the soul." But it is clear Elijah is suddenly wondering: "What have I gotten myself into?" The supremely confident prophet of chapter 18 has become a terrified, fearful, doubting wreck, fleeing into the wilderness.

He falls down beneath the shade of a broom tree, and he says to God: "Take my life." And God does, but not the way Elijah expects. When Elijah says, "take my life," he means: "let me die." But notice there is another way to interpret that phrase. Take my life, God. Take it into your hands, into your care, into your service. That's what God does. God answers Elijah, but not exactly the way Elijah expects.

An angel appears and gives Elijah food and water. He rests. He eats again and then journeys forty days and forty nights in the wilderness until he gets to Mount Horeb. There, he goes into a cave, and sits, and waits.

At this point, you may be picking up some resonances between Elijah and other people in the Bible, especially Moses. Elijah's 40 days and nights in the wilderness are reminiscent of the 40 years Moses spent with the Israelites in the wilderness. And Mount Horeb looms large in the life of Moses, too – it was on Mount Horeb that Moses encountered the Burning Bush, and also, by some accounts the place where he received the Ten Commandments. You also might think of Jesus, and his 40 days in the wilderness at the beginning of his ministry, 40 days during which, like Elijah, angels ministered to him.

Getting back to Elijah there in that cave at Mount Horeb, God now asks Elijah a question: "Why are you here, Elijah?" Although we can only guess at God's tone of voice, I hear this question as a bit of a rebuke. Why are YOU, HERE, Elijah? Why aren't you back where you were, doing my work? What are you doing in a cave in the middle of nowhere?

And in Elijah's answer I hear in a tone of self-pity, an almost pathetic excuse: "I've been very passionate for you, God, because your people have abandoned you. They have torn down your altars and murdered your prophets. I'm the only one left, and now they want to kill me, too. What better place for me to be than here in a cave in the middle of nowhere?"

At this point God realizes how low Elijah has sunk, that he is at the end of his rope. Because God now says: "Go outside, take a deep breath, I'm on my way." And suddenly there is a huge, strong windstorm, and then an earthquake, and then fire. None of which, I imagine, makes Elijah feel any better. And God, we are told, is not "in" any of these big, violent natural events. They are just the announcement of God's coming.

And then there is this "something." After all the wind and earthquake and fire, there is something that is described in three Hebrew words. One of these words means: sound or voice, the second means: a whisper or silence, and the third means: thin or small. You see the problem of putting these three together? There is a bit of a puzzle here, which is why just about every different Bible translation translates these three words differently. The Common English Bible we read today translates each word separately: "a sound. Thin. Quiet." Perhaps the best-known rendering of these three words is: "a still small voice." And my favorite might be: "A sound of sheer silence." The sound of silence. Whatever that means. Whatever it means, it is how God appeared to Elijah, and it brings Elijah out of his cave.

And God and Elijah now repeat, word-for-word, exactly the same conversation they had earlier. Nothing has changed. And yet, somehow, everything has changed.

This time when God asks Elijah: "Why are you here?" I don't hear it as a rebuke, I hear it as a reminder of Elijah's calling, of his purpose. "WHY are you here, Elijah? Think. Remember. Remember who you are, why I called you, and what you been able to do already."

And when Elijah replies, just as before, I don't hear it as self-pity or whining, I hear it as a coming back to himself, so to speak, as a moment of growing realization and remembrance. "I've been very passionate for you, God, because your people have abandoned you. They have torn down your altars and murdered your prophets. I'm the only one left..." Hey, that's right, I'm the only one left to do your work. Here I am, Lord, send me.

And so our passage ends with God saying to Elijah simply: "Go back through the desert to Damascus, there is work to be done, and now you are ready to do it." The passage stops here in the middle of God's speech, but what God tells Elijah to do specifically is go back and anoint some new kings to eventually replace Ahab, and also to pick up his new assistant and successor, Elisha, along the way. Elijah is no longer alone in his work.

It is as if Elijah has been reborn somehow. He was stuck there in his cave and now he has emerged, brought back to life and renewed. We might even say resurrected. That still small voice, that noise, thin and quiet, that sound of sheer silence, whatever it was, gave Elijah back his mojo, he has gotten his groove back, he has rediscovered his purpose and his calling. Perhaps this is how it happened later for Jesus on that first Easter morning – after earthquakes and darkness, God showed up in some quiet but powerful way, spoke a word of silence, and the tomb burst open and Jesus was reborn, much the way Elijah was.

So what does this passage have to say to us? For one thing, I think it reminds us that people of faith, and communities of faith, have their ups and downs, like Elijah. Times when everything seems to be going our way, working out just as we hoped, and other times when things aren't going as well as we'd hoped, when attendance is down, giving is down, when we may feel like we're stuck in a cave in the wilderness all by ourselves. But God is there, God always goes with us. And just when we think all may be lost, that's when God shows up clearly, albeit often quietly, but powerfully, to remind us of our calling and our purpose. I think God's question to Elijah is a good one for us to be asking ourselves as a congregation, every day: Why are we here? WHY are we here, right now? What has God called us to do? And then, we wait, and listen, and look forward to God's answer, which may change everything and give us new life.

Amen.

For Freedom
Galatians 5:1, 13-25

July 7, 2019

On this Sunday after we Americans have celebrated our annual Independence Day and been reminded of the principals that were part of the founding of our country, I want to talk about freedom because that's what Paul talks about in this passage from his letter to the Galatians. Paul is writing more than 1700 years before Thomas Jefferson wrote and the Second Continental Congress approved the Declaration of Independence, so Paul is not talking about freedom from the perspective of an American citizen, but from the perspective of a Christian.

"For freedom Christ has set us free," Paul writes. Our freedom, true freedom, does not come from Thomas Jefferson or any of the Founders, or from any human being or government, but from Christ. And Paul's definition of freedom is very different than the idea of freedom that so many, I fear, were celebrating on July 4th. Many of us have an idea that freedom means we can do whatever we want whenever we want, regardless of how it affects anyone else. This may be freedom in the 21st century American sense but this is not freedom in the Christian sense. As Paul warns: "Do not use your freedom as an opportunity for self-indulgence." Yet so many have the idea that that's exactly what freedom is, self- indulgence. Selfishness. I can do whatever I want.

But according to Paul, Christ has truly set us free, and that freedom brings responsibilities. We have been set free from slavery, slavery to ourselves and our own self-indulgence. Freedom through Christ entails responsibility to others. That is why even though Paul says, "Do not submit again to a yoke of slavery," he goes on to say: "But through love become slaves to one another." Christ removes our yoke of selfishness and self-centeredness, and sets us free to love, and not just to love ourselves but to love others.

Freedom through Christ is the freedom to live in community, to "love your neighbor as yourself." Self-indulgence and self-centeredness only lead us humans to "bite and devour one another," in Paul's words. I fear that phrase sums up all too well the United States here in 2019, as people seem more and more willing to bite each other's heads off and devour each other. Like in that old nursery rhyme: *"There once were two cats of Kilkenny; Each though these was one cat too many; So they fought and they fit, they scratched and they bit; Til, excepting their nails and the tips of their tails; Instead of two cats, there weren't any."*

Paul also reminds us that when it comes to lofty ideas like "freedom," our principals and ideas often far exceed our actions. Which brings me back to Thomas Jefferson. Jefferson, who so famously wrote those lofty words of liberty: "We hold these truths to be self-evident, that all men are created equal, that they are endowed by their Creator with certain unalienable Rights, that among these are Life, Liberty, and the pursuit of Happiness." Yet even as we admire the sentiment, we also know that it was written by a man who owned slaves and approved by a Congress made up of many men who owned slaves. Some people think this lessens the impact of the words, but for me, the flaws and failings of our Founders make their achievements all the more remarkable, even miraculous. These men who owned slaves could have simply stated that all white males are created equal, but they didn't. Some of them may have interpreted it that way, but they wrote it in a way that meant it was also open to be interpreted to include everyone, every human being. Sure, at the time it was written it did largely apply to just white males who owned property, but over time it expanded to include all white males, and then African American males, and then women, and we are still working to expand that definition today. Sure, Jefferson's life never matched his lofty words, and his ideals got stuck in the economic system of which he was a part, but in some ways, I see Jefferson as the quintessential American, because his life embodies so well the character of our country. We were founded on lofty ideals and we have been trying ever since, and too often failing, to live up to them in our lives and laws.

Which brings me to Frederick Douglass. Douglass, the runaway slave who went on to have an amazing life and career, who became a vocal part and in many ways the face of the Abolitionist movement in the 19th century. Seventy-six years to the day after the Declaration of Independence was approved, Douglass was asked to give a speech about the meaning of that moment and the celebration of it. The date was July 4, 1852. The Civil War was less than nine years away, but nobody knew that. What they did know was that a couple years earlier in 1850, Congress had approved a large legislative package of Compromises to try to avert that future war. One of them was called the Fugitive Slave Law, and it mandated that officials across the country were obligated, by law, to help find and return runaway slaves to their masters. This law also made it a criminal offense for any citizen of the United States to offer aid and assistance, food, shelter, comfort of any kind, to a runaway slave, under punishment of law. With all that in mind, Frederick Douglass stood up to speak that day:

> *"This is the 4th of July. It is the birthday of your National Independence, and of your political freedom. This, to you, is what the Passover was to the emancipated people of God...*
>
> *The blessings in which you, this day, rejoice, are not enjoyed in common. The rich inheritance of justice, liberty, prosperity and independence, bequeathed by your fathers, is shared by you, not by me. The sunlight that brought life and healing to you, has brought stripes and death to me. This Fourth [of] July is yours, not mine. You may rejoice, I must mourn...*

Fellow-citizens; above your national, tumultuous joy, I hear the mournful wail of millions! whose chains, heavy and grievous yesterday, are, to-day, rendered more intolerable by the jubilee shouts that reach them… I do not hesitate to declare, with all my soul, that the character and conduct of this nation never looked blacker to me than on this 4th of July! Whether we turn to the declarations of the past, or to the professions of the present, the conduct of the nation seems equally hideous and revolting. America is false to the past, false to the present, and solemnly binds herself to be false to the future…

What, to the American slave, is your 4th of July? I answer: a day that reveals to him, more than all other days in the year, the gross injustice and cruelty to which he is the constant victim. To him, your celebration is a sham; your boasted liberty, an unholy license; your national greatness, swelling vanity; your sounds of rejoicing are empty and heartless; your denunciations of tyrants, brass fronted impudence; your shouts of liberty and equality, hollow mockery; your prayers and hymns, your sermons and thanksgivings, with all your religious parade, and solemnity, are, to him, mere bombast, fraud, deception, impiety, and hypocrisy— a thin veil to cover up crimes which would disgrace a nation of savages. There is not a nation on the earth guilty of practices, more shocking and bloody, than are the people of these United States, at this very hour…

At the very moment that they are thanking God for the enjoyment of civil and religious liberty, and for the right to worship God according to the dictates of their own consciences, they are utterly silent in respect to a law which robs religion of its chief significance…Did this law concern the "mint, anise and cummin"—abridge the right to sing psalms, to partake of the sacrament, or to engage in any of the ceremonies of religion, it would be smitten by the thunder of a thousand pulpits. A general shout would go up from the church, demanding repeal, repeal, instant repeal! Further, if this demand were not complied with, another Scotland would be added to the history of religious liberty, and the stern old Covenanters would be thrown into the shade. A John Knox would be seen at every church door, and heard from every pulpit, and Fillmore would have no more quarter than was shown by Knox, to the beautiful, but treacherous queen Mary of Scotland. The fact that the church of our country... does not esteem "the Fugitive Slave Law" as a declaration of war against religious liberty, implies that that church regards religion simply as a form of worship, an empty ceremony, and not a vital principle, requiring active benevolence, justice, love and good will towards man. It esteems sacrifice above mercy; psalm-singing above right doing; solemn meetings above practical righteousness. A worship that can be conducted by persons who refuse to give shelter to the houseless, to give bread to the hungry, clothing to the naked, and who enjoin obedience to a law forbidding these acts of mercy, is a curse, not a blessing to mankind...

But the church of this country is not only indifferent to the wrongs of the slave, it actually takes sides with the oppressors. It has made itself the bulwark of American slavery, and the shield of American slave-hunters. Many of its most eloquent Divines. who stand as the very lights of the church, have shamelessly given the sanction of religion and the Bible to the whole slave system. They have taught that man may, properly, be a slave; that the relation of master and slave is ordained of God; that to send back an escaped bondman to his master is clearly the duty of all the followers of the Lord Jesus Christ; and this horrible blasphemy is palmed off upon the world for Christianity.

These ministers make religion a cold and flinty-hearted thing, having neither principles of right action, nor bowels of compassion. They strip the love of God of its beauty, and leave the throng of religion a huge, horrible, repulsive form. It is a religion for oppressors, tyrants, man-stealers, and thugs. But a religion which favors the rich against the poor; which exalts the proud above the humble; which divides mankind into two classes, tyrants and slaves; which says to the man in chains, stay there; and to the oppressor, oppress on; it is a religion which may be professed and

> *enjoyed by all the robbers and enslavers of mankind; it makes God a respecter of persons, denies his fatherhood of the race, and tramples in the dust the great truth of the brotherhood of man...*
>
> *You boast of your love of liberty, your superior civilization, and your pure Christianity, while the whole political power of the nation (as embodied in the two great political parties), is solemnly pledged to support and perpetuate the enslavement of three millions of your countrymen...You profess to believe "that, of one blood, God made all nations of men to dwell on the face of all the earth," and hath commanded all men, everywhere to love one another; yet you notoriously hate, (and glory in your hatred), all men whose skins are not colored like your own.*
>
> *Fellow-citizens! I will not enlarge further on your national inconsistencies. The existence of slavery in this country brands your republicanism as a sham, your humanity as a base pretense, and your Christianity as a lie. It destroys your moral power abroad; it corrupts your politicians at home. It saps the foundation of religion; it makes your name a hissing, and a by word to a mocking earth...It fetters your progress; it is the enemy of improvement, the deadly foe of education; it fosters pride; it breeds insolence; it promotes vice; it shelters crime; it is a curse to the earth that supports it; and yet, you cling to it, as if it were the sheet anchor of all your hopes."*

Douglass is expressing something very similar to what Paul does: "Far too often your actions do not align with your professed beliefs." We have outlawed slavery, at least the form Douglass knew, but there is still plenty of oppression in our country and our world today. As Americans, we proclaim liberty and freedom - how are we doing at living these beliefs as Americans? As Christians, we proclaim love and justice – how are we doing at living these beliefs as Christians?

On this Independence Day weekend, the words of Paul of Tarsus and Thomas Jefferson and Frederick Douglass ring in my ears, offering a profound and powerful and uncomfortable reminder to us as Christians, that we will only be truly free if we are working to ensure than every single child of God on earth is equally free and able to enjoy the God-given blessings of life, liberty, and the pursuit of happiness.

Amen.

A Commandment Very Close to Us
Luke 10:25-37; Deuteronomy 30:9-14

July 14, 2019

The parable of the Good Samaritan is probably one of the most, if not the most, familiar of all Jesus's parables. Even people who have never been to church know the reference if you refer to someone as a "good Samaritan." The problem with things that are that familiar, especially Bible passages, is that we are so used to them, so familiar with them, feel so comfortable with them, that we may miss what they really say because we just assume after hearing them so often that we already know what they say. That's why it always good to revisit familiar passages of Scripture like this one, to be reminded what exactly is going on and being said, not just in the parable but in the even more interesting story that surrounds it.

But first some comments about Samaritans. This is one of the aspects of this parable that can be toughest for us as 21st century Americans to really grasp, the depth of the hatred between the Jews and Samaritans the lies behind this parable. Why did they hate each other so much? The answer is not entirely clear, but there are clues offered for us in other places in Scripture. The Samaritans first appear in 2 Kings chapter 17, after the Assyrians have invaded and taken over the northern kingdom of Israel. Many of the Jews in that region were exiled to Assyria, and so the vacuum left there was filled by the Assyrians with people from other places, like Mesopotamia, who settled in Samaria. Now these new "Samaritans" were not worshippers of Yahweh, the Hebrew God, and interestingly, the Book of Second Kings informs us that God sent lions to roam the area and kill the people for that reason. The Assyrians got wise to this and they imported some Hebrew priests who know Yahweh and Yahweh's laws to teach all this to the new people living there. So the Samaritans began to follow Jewish laws and worship regulations to some degree, but they also maintained their worship of the gods they brought with them from Mesopotamia. They also did not look to the Temple in Jerusalem as the center of their faith, but they essentially built their own Temple on Mount Gerizim. I don't know if this is where the animosity between the Jews and Samaritans begins, but if it doesn't begin at that point, the books of Ezra and Nehemiah both insinuate that the Samaritans were among those who opposed the rebuilding of the Temple in Jerusalem after the Jewish exiles from Babylon returned. The point is, however this animosity began, by the time we jump ahead centuries and centuries to the time of Jesus, the Samaritans were absolutely detested, perhaps because they were very close to the Hebrew people, even in terms of their religion, but with slight yet meaningful differences. Often the people we have the most trouble with are the ones closest to us, maybe even in our own families—people very much like us but with slight yet, to us, meaningful differences.

Let me read to you some thoughts by the writer and scholar Amy Jill-Levine, who is Jewish and who writes to help us Christians better understand that part of our own heritage, about the Samaritans: *"We should think of ourselves as the person in the ditch and then ask, "Is there anyone from any group, about whom we'd rather die than [accept help]? More, is there any group whose members might rather die than help us? Is so, then we know how to find the modern equivalent for the Samaritan."* Levine goes on to remark that for herself as Jewish woman, she often envisions the Samaritan as a member of the Palestinian group Hamas. Or she suggests we Americans in the wake of 9/11 might imagine the Samaritan as a member of Al-Qaeda, or I'd suggest more recently perhaps a member of ISIS or a neo-Nazi, or maybe even that one member of your own family who, at family reunions, you will not even cross the room to speak to. That's the symbolism of this Samaritan, a person or member of a group that we would go to great lengths to avoid any contact with.

So the story in Luke begins with this legal expert coming to Jesus and asking a pretty good question: "What must I do to gain eternal life?"

Jesus, in good rabbinic fashion, answers his question with another question: "What does Torah say?"

The legal expert knows his Torah, and he says: "Love God with all your heart and mind and strength and love your neighbor as yourself."

And Jesus says: "Excellent answer. Go and do this and live." Which is in and of itself a pretty good sermon.

But the legal expert starts asking more questions. Questions are generally a good thing, but sometimes they can simply be a way of delaying having to do what you've just been told to do. Jesus has been pretty clear what the legal expert needs to do: "Love God and love you neighbor as yourself. Do that and live." That's pretty clear cut. The legal expert, I think, wants to avoid all the implications of that answer. To him that sounds like a tall order, maybe a bit unreasonable, even though it is clearly stated in Torah. So he keeps asking further questions. Maybe for clarification, but I suspect more to avoid what he has already been told.

The legal expert asks: "Who is my neighbor? If I'm commanded to love my neighbor as myself, who exactly is my neighbor?"

Notice the implication of this question. What the legal expert really wants to know is: What are the limits here? What are the boundaries? He's a legal expert so I think he is hoping Jesus will say: "Well, according to the law, section 108.32-12, a neighbor is defined as anyone who lives within a 1.8-mile radius of you, measured from the center of your dining room." A very precise definition with clear, quantifiable limits. What are the limits of who I have to help, what are the precise boundaries of love? That's what the legal expert wants to know. This reminds me of that time Peter asked Jesus: "How often do I have to forgive? Seven times?" What are the precise boundaries for my having to forgive? The legal expert, like Peter, wants to know the limits of love.

So Jesus tells the parable of the Good Samaritan.

And we all know the parable: a man, presumably a Jew, is travelling from Jerusalem down to Jericho. I didn't realize until I visited Israel ten years ago why the story says the man was going "down." It's about altitude. Jerusalem is up on a hill, and Jericho is down by the Jordan River and the Dead Sea, and to get to Jericho you do, literally, go down, quite steeply. Also worth mentioning is that even today, or at least as of 2009 when I was there, there are portions of this 20-something mile journey that goes through desert and desolate wilderness. Along his journey, this man is beset by thieves and robbers, they strip him naked, take all his possessions, leave him for dead, bleeding and wounded there in a ditch. A priest happens to come walking by, sees the man in the ditch, moves across the road and continues on his way. A Levite, another religious leader, comes walking by, sees the man in the ditch, moves across the road and continues on his way. Then a Samaritan comes by, sees the man in the ditch, has compassion for him, goes to him, binds his wounds, takes him on his donkey to the nearest inn, pays the innkeeper, says: "Give this man the best care possible, here's a bunch of money, and I will stop by on my way back through this area and if there is any additional cost for this man's care, I will pay it then."

Now remember, that Jewish man in the ditch would have much preferred that the priest or the Levite stop and help, and if he had had his say, he probably would have said: "There's no way I want a Samaritan to help me. I'd rather die first." But it is the Samaritan who helps.

Jesus finishes telling his parable, and then poses a question to the legal expert, a very different question than the one the legal expert initially posed to him. The initial question asked was: "Who is my neighbor?" Jesus now asks: "Which one of the three was a neighbor? Who behaved like a neighbor in this parable?" Do you hear the difference in those questions? Jesus turns the legal expert's question on its head; we've gone from "what is the limit of who I have to love," to "who acted most like a neighbor?" Not "Who is my neighbor?" but "How can I be a neighbor?" And of course the legal expert has to acknowledge that the hated Samaritan was the one who behaved like a neighbor, was the one who showed mercy, who demonstrated love.

Jesus says: "Excellent answer. Go and do it." Stop wondering who your neighbor might be and go and be a neighbor. To everyone.

This is where I want to bring in the passage from Deuteronomy, where Moses is telling the people, as he does throughout the entire book of Deuteronomy: "Don't forget the Lord. Remember the Lord. Obey the Lord's commandments. Keep God's word close to you." When Moses says that God's word is close, in their mouths and hearts, he is speaking literally, which is why the orthodox Jews wear phylacteries, small boxes with portions of Torah in them, on their arms and on their foreheads, and why they put mezuzahs, small cases with readings from Torah in them, on their doorposts. They keep God's word that close.

But in reference to this parable, I think there is an interesting twist to these words of Moses. "Keep the commandment to love close to you." You don't have to cross the ocean to fulfill this commandment, you don't need to wait for someone to come down from heaven to provide you opportunities to love. This commandment to love may take a lifetime to master, but it not too difficult to begin doing. The opportunities to begin living this commandment are close to us. Very close.

I want you to turn right now to the person or person sitting closest to you this morning. Go ahead, this is the audience participation portion of this sermon. Turn to the person sitting closest to you, beside you or in front or behind you. Keep looking at them, don't be shy. The people you are looking at are where you begin fulfilling the commandment to love. And in the week ahead whoever comes within that 1.8-mile range of you also provides a continual source of opportunities for you to fulfill this commandment to love. The opportunities for us to demonstrate love, to be a neighbor, are right here, close to us – they are in our own backyards, they are in our own pews, they are in our own families, they are in our own communities, and they extend far, far beyond as well. There is no limit to them, but they start very close to each one of us.

We don't have to look far to fulfill this commandment, to live out the moral of this parable, to be a good neighbor. So keep looking.

Look and do, love and live.

Amen.

II. Snapshots from the Church Year

Good Old Zephaniah
Zephaniah 3:14-20

December 16, 2018

We don't hear from old Zephaniah that often. There may be some of you who didn't even know there was a prophet named Zephaniah, or you might easily confuse him with Zechariah. Poor Zephaniah doesn't get much respect, he's the Rodney Dangerfield of the Biblical prophets, I suppose. But Zephaniah was prophesying at an interesting time in the history of the Hebrew people. We don't know much about Zephaniah the man except what is in his book. We're told who some of his ancestors were, and it is thought he might even have been, Egyptian, but we do know he was writing at the time of King Josiah. This was a moment in the history of Israel and Judah that was fraught with a lot of anxiety. The Assyrian empire was not as strong as it once had been, the Assyrians who had come down from the north and not quite captured Jerusalem, they had been driven back at the last minute. But they were still out there, lurking. Meanwhile there was another empire, this one centered in Babylon, growing as well, and the Babylonian Empire would become a bigger threat in the next century. Of course there may not ever have been a time in history given the geographic position of Israel in which there wasn't some empire waiting to come through their land, so it does seem that this part of the world has always been filled with tension and uncertainty and anxiety – what next?

But at this particular moment there was also hope. King Josiah is often held up as the last great king of Judah. He decreed and implemented a number of reforms in the nation but also in the Temple and the religious institutions of the time. It was during the time of King Josiah that the Book of Deuteronomy and those laws and regulations therein were discovered, actually rediscovered, and Josiah worked hard to implement them and to bring the people and their institutions back to faithful obedience to God's laws.

So Zephaniah is prophesying at a time of great anxiety but also great hopefulness, perhaps not unlike our time. Perhaps not unlike ALL times.

It is worth noting, I think, that there are two commands offered by Zephaniah in today's passage: Rejoice, and Do Not Fear.

No matter what may be going on in your world, in your life, no matter what anxiety you may be feeling, rejoice. And do not fear. This is very much an Advent message. Rejoice, and do not fear.

But Zephaniah is not offering a Pollyanna-ish, pie-in-the-sky-by-and-by theology here. He tells us why we are to rejoice and not fear. He says rejoice and do not fear because the Lord is in your midst. That is truly an Advent reminder. I've mentioned in previous sermons that Advent is a season that transcends time and the flow of time. You may remember the words from the Book of Revelation we read a few weeks ago that describe the Lord as the one who "was and is and is coming". Zephaniah has that same feel to his writing, transcending, even embracing, ALL times. The bottom line of this passage is that it is all about what God has done, what God is doing, and what God will do. In Advent, all of this comes together. This interesting season when we are waiting to celebrate in the future something that has already happened: the birth of Jesus. And we are also waiting for what has yet to happen: the coming of Jesus again. Yet that event which is yet to happen is already happening and so Advent is this weird season in which we live in ALL times at once as we await the Lord who transcends and is outside of time itself. And Zephaniah reminds us that this same Lord is within our midst, right here, right now. You are waiting, you are preparing, and yet God is with you, the Lord is with you already. Somehow Advent invites us to hold all of this together. No matter what may be going on in our world and in our lives, to know with certainty, even as we wait, that what we are waiting for is not just certain but is already happening: The Lord is here.

These are the kinds of theological paradoxes I enjoy pondering on snowy days at home while sitting with my cat Fred on my lap.

Something else caught my attention in this passage. Zephaniah is not just reminding us that the Lord is in our midst, he then begins to describe the Lord, the one who is coming but is already here. He describes the Lord as a warrior who is bringing victory. Now that may perk us up a bit! Finally, the Lord is coming as a warrior, bringing victory, like John Wayne or Clint Eastwood riding into town, the way many of the Hebrew people expected the Messiah to come, on a white horse with a flaming sword to kill, to utterly wipe out, all our enemies or at least all of God's enemies—and of course we know those two groups are always exactly the same, right?

But lest we get too caught up in the warrior image, notice what Zephaniah says immediately after he says the Lord is coming like a warrior bringing victory: he brings "calm with his love" and rejoicing with singing. The Lord comes to gather the outcasts and deliver the lame. To bring us all, ALL, back to God.

What kind of crazy, mixed-up warrior is this?

A warrior who brings calm with his love? That sure doesn't sound like John Wayne (no offense to John Wayne).

What kind of warrior is this bringing calm and love? It gets even stranger when you realize the Hebrew word here translated "calm" can also mean "to soothe" with his love. This is a warrior who comes to soothe people's wounds and bring peace, maybe even bring goodwill on earth. This is a warrior who comes bringing a victory for all of those who are outcast and overlooked, poor and homeless and suffering. This is a warrior who comes not swinging a sword, but swinging with song, more Frank Sinatra than Clint Eastwood.

This is the Lord we await at Advent, but who is already in our midst: a Lord of calm and love and peace and song, a Lord of deliverance to bring us back to God, not at the point of a sword, but with calming, soothing words of peace.

How many of you are hungry for some soothing words and moments of calm this time of year? Well, that is the gift the Lord brings us. That's what we wait for at Advent, but what we also acknowledge is already here, if we help make it be here.

One commentator I was reading while preparing this week's sermon was writing three years ago, in Advent 2015, the last time this passage appeared in the 3-year cycle of the lectionary. This person was commenting on the political season that had already started at that point as the 2016 election was already in full swing, and with it all of the *sturm and drang* associated with elections which even then seemed so divisive and full of fear, and this writer commented about this passage, and I'm paraphrasing slightly: Boy, we really need old Zephaniah this year. I'd suggest to you that has not changed, and in fact perhaps we need Zephaniah even more now than we did three years ago. Boy do we need old Zephaniah this year, right now. With a message about the Lord who is coming to bring love and calm and hope and deliverance, to gather all people together and bring them back together to God. Boy do we need old Zephaniah to remind us of what we are supposed to be focusing most of our efforts on in this Advent season: Rejoicing, and not being afraid. Good old Zephaniah. Maybe we'll learn how to do better before we hear from him again in another 3 years.

Amen.

I've Looked at Clouds From Both Sides Now
Psalm 99; Luke 9:28-36

March 3, 2019

I started the week pondering God's voice and how God speaks to us. By the end of the week I was pondering clouds.

Did you notice how clouds figure prominently in both our readings for this Transfiguration Sunday?

The cloud appears in the latter part of the Transfiguration story in Luke, so it is easy to miss. Jesus goes up on a mountaintop with Peter, James, and John, and while praying there he is revealed in all his divine glory. I love how this translation describes his clothes as flashing white like lightning, like a strobe light. Jesus is revealed in all his holiness and divinity. Moses and Elijah appear, and the three disciples don't know exactly what to do. Peter chimes up with an idea that they should build some shrines, and then the cloud descends around them. From within the cloud, a voice speaks to them – presumably God, the same voice who spoke to Jesus at his baptism. Here the voice speaks to the disciples, and it tells them: "This is my Son, listen to him!" The cloud lifts, Jesus is once again back to normal and alone, and the disciples are rendered speechless.

In our Psalm this morning, God also speaks from a cloud. In this Psalm which speaks of God's holiness and majesty and divinity, which reminds us to bow down and magnify God, we are also reminded about God's prophets Moses and Aaron and Samuel, that God answered them when they called, that God spoke to them from a "pillar of cloud."

This is obviously a reference to the exodus, when the Israelites wandered in the wilderness for 40 years and God went with them, leading them as a pillar of cloud by day and a pillar of fire by night. There are many examples of God speaking to God's people in and from a cloud like this. When Moses went up to Mount Sinai to talk to God, a cloud covered the mountain and Moses disappeared into it. That's why the people got scared after 40 days and made a golden calf idol. When the prophet Elijah was taken up into heaven, he was taken up in a cloud, a whirlwind. Perhaps that's why he and Moses appear with Jesus in the Transfiguration – they are both familiar with being in God's cloud. But the examples go on. God's presence is often signaled by a cloud. When Solomon finally builds the Temple in Jerusalem, and the people gather to consecrate the hold space, God's presence descends in a cloud, just as God led the people in a cloud and spoke them from a cloud. So why is God's presence, God's voice, represented so often by a cloud?

While pondering that question, I was reminded of driving in fog. Last weekend I drove to a conference and the day was a miserable one, weather-wise. Gray and rainy and misty, and part of my drive, that stretch down the mountain from Spruce Pine to Marion, was in dense fog. Whenever I drive in fog my neck aches and my shoulders hurt from being all tensed up and leaning forward to try to see my way. Fog requires us to pay attention, more attention than usual.

Fog makes us pay more attention than usual. Maybe that's why God speaks from the cloud, maybe that's why the cloud descended on the disciples at the Transfiguration, because with all their other senses gone, they had to listen to God, they had no other choice. In the cloud you can't see as clearly as you might like.

That gets us to the second aspect of the cloud, and perhaps to the deeper meaning of God being revealed in and speaking from the cloud: the cloud doesn't make things clearer, but cloudier. The cloud takes away our certainty and opens us to God's voice. So often we get convinced of our own certainty, convinced we have the answers, that we have it all figured out. But then the cloud of God descends and reminds us that we don't, that things are not as simple, as black and white, as either/or as we might think.

Listen to him, God says about Jesus. And Jesus tells us to love, but that is never as simple as it might sound. "Do good," Jesus says, but that is never as simple as it sounds. When we begin to try to apply that to real, everyday life, it gets more complex; once you start trying to live love and goodness, things get cloudy quickly. But maybe that's what it means to grow in faith, to mature in faith – to begin to see that life and love and following Christ are not as simple and easy as we might have once thought.

I think that is one of the big problems in our world today, especially in this country. Too many people think they have it all figured out, think they see things clearer than anyone else, are certain they know the solution. It seems so simple, so obvious to them. Thus the rabid polarization of people so certain they know the answers, and that anyone who thinks otherwise is wrong. But the world's big problems are almost always more complex than we think, and they are solved by coming together in the middle, through compromise, acknowledging that no person or group has a lock on the whole answer.

At the Transfiguration, Peter thought he had things all figured out. He has that moment when he is certain he knows why Jesus has brought him and his fellow disciples. "It is good we are here," he says. "We should construct three shrines, one for you, and one for Moses and one for Elijah. Now I know why you brought three of us, one for each of you who has appeared here on the mountaintop, each of us to build a shrine." Peter is certain he knows the solution, that he sees clearly. Then the cloud descends. Then God speaks. And the disciples learn wisdom in that cloud – the wisdom of humility, the wisdom of speechlessness, of keeping their mouths shut and listening. Things aren't as clear-cut and certain as they thought.

God is holy, as Psalm 99 keeps reminding us. God is great and holy and divine and mysterious, and just when we think we have God all figured out, God reminds us that God is revealed not in certainty but in uncertainty. That's the great paradox of this moment of the Transfiguration—this moment when Jesus is revealed in all his divine glory doesn't make things clearer and simpler for us, it really makes things harder and more complex. Maybe we have to be willing, as followers of Jesus Christ, to dwell in the cloud rather than start building shrines to our own certainty. Because acknowledging how little we really know and understand means relying on God, trusting in God. This moment of Transfiguration reveals that our certainty is an illusion, and that all we have to fall back on in the fog of life is our faith, our trust in God. Maybe beginning to truly understand that is what it means to be truly transfigured by God.

Amen.

All in the Family
Joel 2:12-17; Romans 10:8b-13

March 10, 2019

These two passages of Scripture are perfect for getting us started on our journey through the season of Lent. They both remind us of what this season is about and keep us focused on what is truly important as we journey towards Easter.

Let me start with the prophet Joel and his reminder to us, more than once, that our task is to "return" to God. "Return to me," God says, "return to the Lord your God." Joel reminds us that this season of confession and humility is centered on repentance, which literally means to "turn toward God." Joel reminds us that we are called to return to God. One can only return to someplace one has already been. Our sin and separation from God are not our original state of being. Whether you take the story of Adam and Eve and the garden literally or as a metaphor for the human condition, the message is really the same - at one time we were close to God, with God, made, indeed in God's image. But we have fallen away from that state of being. We have given in to the lesser angels of our nature, we have gotten to a point, as human beings, where everything we touch, we screw up. But that is not our original state, that is not what God intended for us. And so Joel, and the season of Lent, invites us to return, to go back, to being more the kind of people God wants and hopes we might be.

This return involves a change of heart. Did you notice all the references to the heart in these readings? Joel says we should return to the Lord with "all our hearts," and that we should "tear" our hearts, not our clothes. Paul says that we should confess "in our hearts" and trust with our hearts and have faith in our hearts. Part of our Lenten journey is to change our hearts, to retune and return our hearts to God, the one who first made them.

But Joel also poses an interesting question. Even as we are trying to change our hearts, Joel asks: "Who knows whether God will have a change of heart?" We know that we need a change of heart, but does God need a change of heart, too? Who knows? Well Paul claims we do know the answer to that question. Will God have a change of heart? The answer, according to Paul, is "no." God doesn't have to have a change of heart because God's heart never left us. God doesn't have to return to us, because God never left. God loves us. That has never changed. There is nothing we can do to earn God's love because we have never been without it. That's important to remember in this season of Lent. Even as we confess and fast and weep, even as we return to God and try to change our hearts, we don't do any of this for God's benefit, we do it for our benefit. We don't do any of this to force God to get closer to us or to return to us. God has always been here. God has always loved us. ALL of us.

Did you notice the number of times that Paul uses that word "all" in this short passage from Romans? There is no distinction between people in God's eyes, because the same Lord is Lord of all. The same Lord gives richly to all. Notice that Joel mentions gathering the people, all the people: old people, young people, even nursing infants, brides and grooms and even priests. Where is their God? God is among the people, all the people. Old and young, black and white, Jew and Gentiles, Republican and Democrat and Independent. God's love is for all people. And all who call on the Lord's name will be saved. Christ came to save all people, and all who have faith in that simple fact, all who trust in God, all who call out to the

Lord, who desire to be saved, will be saved. All of them. No exceptions.

Now I can hear what some of you might be saying: "Preacher, does that mean that Hitler is saved? That Stalin is saved? That Ghengis Khan is saved? That Osama Bin Laden is saved?"

Well, let me tell you…I don't know! Why would you expect me to know that? That is far above my pay grade, not to mention none of my business, or yours, either. It is not up to any of us to determine who is saved. Besides, if someday you get to walk through the gates of heaven and the first person you see standing there is Hitler, what are you going to do? Walk back out? I do know that Paul declares that ALL who call upon the name of the Lord will be saved. That ALL who trust in the Lord in their hearts will be saved. I also know that God is God, and God can save anyone God wants to. That's enough for me. Anything beyond that is really none of my concern. Because as we start this season of Lent, I've got some important work of my own to focus on…and so do you. We ALL do.

Amen.

Our Heavenly Gardener
Psalm 63:1-8; Luke 13:1-9

March 24, 2019

It has been another week of bad news, especially natural disasters. More and more that seems to be the case every single week, and I don't see that changing anytime soon. Often in the wake of such disasters, there are those among us who look for someone to blame, and a few people who blame the victims themselves, who claim that God is punishing them, that they deserved what they got. This is nothing new, as our gospel reading this morning clearly shows.

It begins with Jesus responding to some people in Jerusalem have been talking about some recent disasters – some Galileans killed by the Roman forces under Pontius Pilate, and others killed when the tower of Siloam fell on them. Jesus raises the challenging question for these rumor mongers: "Do you think that you are better than these people who were killed? Do you think they were worse than you are? No, I tell you: you are all going to die." Well, Gee – thanks for that pleasant reminder, Jesus.

Actually though, Jesus is making a deeper point. He's distinguishing between physical death, which we all will experience eventually, whether we want to think about it or not, and spiritual death, which we may not have to experience. We are all going to die a physical death, but Jesus says that if we "change our hearts and lives" we may avoid spiritual death. And of the two kinds of death, spiritual death is worse…much worse.

As much as we dread physical death I suspect most if not all of us are even more fearful of spiritual death - of being cut off from the Divine. I think we all long for spiritual life, a life of purpose, a life with meaning beyond ourselves, a life of satisfaction and accomplishment and love. I think we all long to be satisfied and made whole. This is what I hear Psalm 63 saying to God: "I seek you; I thirst for you, my whole being longs for you." I hear echoes of Saint Augustine who said: "Our hearts are restless until they rest in you, O God." Too often our modern world feels dry and lifeless, and we are like thirsty people in a dry and parched and barren wilderness, spiritually. Or that's how it feels.

I think that brings us to the fig tree. That fig tree in the parable Jesus tells about the owner of a vineyard, within which is a fig tree. The owner has been waiting for three years and yet the tree has yet to produce even one, solitary fig. In frustration the owner goes to the gardener and says: "I've had it! I've wasted three long years on this tree, lots of resources, good soil, and gotten nothing in return. Cut it down!" The gardener, though, pleads for the tree. "Give it a little more time. I will pay special attention to it, I will tend it, water it, even fertilize it. Give it another season to bear fruit."

This is a parable about grace and patience. The grace of the gardener, and the patience, even if reluctant, of the vineyard owner. The tree gets more time. It seems pretty clear that the tree is us. You and me, individually but maybe also our entire human family. Maybe the world itself. And the gardener is clearly Jesus, gracious, loving, forgiving Jesus, who pleads on our behalf. Which means, perhaps, but I'm less clear about this, that the owner of the vineyard is God or at least one aspect of God, because remember the gardener, if it is Jesus, is also God. Do you ever think though how exasperated God must get with us, his creation? How frustrated we must make God sometimes? Because God has given us everything and we keep messing it up – we keep letting our doubts and our fears get in our way. We keep failing to bear the fruit of love and peace and joy and hope and goodness and failing in a big way.

In the past I've always thought the message of this parable was that we trees were being given a little more time, one more chance, by God to try to produce some fruit. To force out one little fig, at least. But recently I began wondering – can a tree will itself to produce fruit? That question made me consider that this parable isn't really a parable about a tree; it is really all about the gardener. The tree doesn't do or say anything in this parable. It is the gardener who does everything. It is the gardener who pleads on behalf of the tree. It is the gardener who promises to do all the work – to tend the tree, to lavish it with special attention, to water it, to feed it, even to fertilize it. The tree needs this gardener, and the gardener is going to do everything the tree needs. That's what Jesus does for us, of course. That's what Lent is guiding us towards – Good Friday and Easter and their reminder of the lengths and depths to which Jesus is willing to go for us.

Jesus is our true gardener, the one who promises to give us everything we need. To water us and satisfy our thirst, to feed us, as with a rich feast, to tend to us with tender loving care, more love than we could ever desire. Jesus says he will give us everything we need to grow and bear fruit, but that may be different than what we want. It won't be pleasant every step of the way. There's fertilizer involved, for one thing. Fertilizer, which we here in an agricultural area know means…manure. I wonder if a tree getting manure put around it ever wants to complain about the smell. But it is necessary for growth, and sometimes Jesus sends some manure our way, something that we may not like the smell of – love you enemy, for example. Or welcome the foreigner, visit the prisoner, care for the widow and the orphan and the poor. These things might not smell very good according to our modern world's view. But this fertilizer is necessary for our growth, and for us to bear fruit.

The parable doesn't mention pruning, but pruning is also essential for a tree to bear fruit, and there are other passages of scripture that allude to Jesus pruning us, too. Cutting off some of those useless branches, suckers they are called, cutting short our attempts to branch out in the direction we want to go, to do something we want to do, but that is not in our best interest, so we can focus our energy on bearing good fruit.

As we continue our journey through Lent together, I am thinking these passages might be reminding of the importance of our Heavenly Gardener, who not only is full of grace, but is filling us with everything we need to bear good fruit, whether we want it or not. Perhaps that is what Jesus means when he talks about "changing our hearts and lives." Perhaps that is what it means to truly repent, to turn, to turn back to Jesus, our gardener. Because there are a lot of people who claim to be spiritual gardeners in our world today. Fake gardeners, false shepherds, who claim to know what is best for us. "Let me tend you. Just listen to me, let me solve all your problems." But then we discover they want something from us, usually our money or our vote. But Jesus says: here I am, your true gardener, your good gardener, your heavenly gardener. Remember me, turn back to me, let me give you want you truly need to be satisfied. Maybe part of our Lenten journey is to let ourselves be tended to by him, to be fed and pruned and loved. To let ourselves bear fruit, before God's patience and fertilizer run out.

Amen.

The Spirit of Understanding
Romans 8:12-17; Acts 2:1-21

June 9, 2019

On this Pentecost Sunday, I think it is worth starting my reflections with a nice, deep breath, since the Hebrew word for spirit, "ruah," is also the word for breath and also wind. So please join me in a deep breath as we begin.

Now I'd like to reflect on what exactly the breath of the Holy Spirit brought to the people there in Jerusalem that day, and, more importantly, on what the Holy Spirit offers to us here in the modern world for the work we are called to do.

It is worth remembering why the people were gathered in Jerusalem that day. Pentecost was a Jewish holy day before it became a Christian one. It was known as the Feast of Weeks, or in Hebrew, "Shavuot," and although it began as an agricultural festival, by the time of Jesus it had become a celebration of that moment when God gave Moses the Law, the Torah, there on Mount Sinai. Thus it is both fitting and ironic that this festival celebrating the moment when the Jewish people became the Chosen People of God also serves as the birthday of the Christian Church, that moment when, with the coming of the Holy Spirit, it began to grow into the institution it eventually became, for better or for worse. But back to the account in Acts: because of this festival, there are Jews in Jerusalem from all over the world, and as they are gathered, suddenly there is a sound like the rush of wind, and tongues, as of fire, appear over their heads, and the people start talking, preaching, proclaiming, in languages that everyone can understand. It is commonly thought that the miracle of Pentecost is a miracle of speaking, but I am reminded of a professor of mine in seminary who suggested to us that perhaps the real miracle was a miracle of hearing, not speaking. Notice how many times it is stated in Acts 2 that the people were amazed to be hearing others speaking in their own native language. And I think the Spirit that descended upon the crowd that day in Jerusalem brought not just the miracle of speaking and the miracle of hearing, but above all the miracle of understanding. The Holy Spirit is a Spirit of understanding.

It occurs to me that one of the biggest things we lack in today's world, especially here in this country, is a spirit of understanding.

This is where Paul's commentary on the work of the Spirit is instructive. In Romans 8, Paul is not directly commenting on Pentecost, but he does offer some insightful description on the Holy Spirit that descended that day and which still guides us. That Spirit, Paul declares, bestows upon each one of us an obligation, not an obligation of selfishness, away from others, but an obligation of love, of living towards and with others. Yet it seems like our society today is living more and more selfishly, focused on ourselves, putting ourselves first. Paul also reminds us that the Holy Spirit is not a Spirit of fear. As people led by God's Spirit, we are not to be led by our own fears but led by love. Again, doesn't it seem like we today are living in a climate of fear, with so many people, politicians and pundits, stoking our fears? Yet Paul declares that God's Holy Spirit is a Spirit of love, not fear; a Spirit of community, not selfishness; a Spirit of life, not of death. All of which is wrapped up in the Spirit promoting understanding, not division.

The irony, the sad, painful irony is that this Spirit is exactly what our world is so sorely in need of today, even as the world seems to be actively working against that Spirit. We have today, for example, at our very fingertips in our devices access to so much knowledge, almost unimaginable the knowledge and data we have available to us, and yet I don't think we are getting any smarter when it comes to living better or living together.

We were promised access to so much knowledge, and yet we lack basic wisdom and common sense. We were promised through technology and social media increased connection, but these very same technologies are what fuel so much hatred and division instead. It is so easy today with these technologies of connection to instead get stuck in your own little bubble, behind walls of your own making. To only encounter people just like you.

The coming of the Holy Spirit at Pentecost, though, brought real connection to people from all over the world. True understanding, through genuine communication. That made all the difference, and began the rapid growth of the early church, bringing people together despite differences, despite diverse backgrounds and beliefs. That is the promise of the early Church and the hope of the Spirit of Understanding.

I belief this gets to the profound and much needed calling of the Christian Church today to be models of understanding and community, to show how people can come together and build bridges across all the barriers that threaten to tear us apart as human beings. I'm not sure there is another institution in our modern world that can truly serve as such an example anymore, except us.

So how do we do that? What does the Spirit of understanding prompt us to do today? What is required for genuine understanding?

One of the first things required to understand someone else is time. It takes time to get to know someone. And it takes more than technology. Real communication and connection cannot be done solely by our electronic devices, through text or email. How many times have you sent someone an email, or a text and they totally misinterpret it because they can't hear your tone of voice or see your body language? Understanding takes time, precious time, face-to-face and person-to-person.

Unfortunately that is another commodity that seems to be sorely lacking in our modern world of busyness – time. I believe the Holy Spirit encourages us to make that time a priority so we can connect with and understand each other.

Secondly, understanding requires openness, an openness to ideas and perspectives different than our own. This requires us to do some exploring, figuring out "why" a person believes or acts the way they do. Why does someone hold a totally opposite view on abortion or immigration than I do? What leads them to that belief? Is it just because they are stupid or evil? Probably not, and certainly not as often as we like to think. The Spirit of understanding encourages us to listen to others, truly listen in order to understand where someone is coming from, what their background is, what experiences they have had, to get to know their story, so we can perhaps better understand their perspective and not so easily dismiss them.

Finally, understanding requires the recognition of what Paul reminds the Romans: "we are God's children," all of us. And not just children of God, but heirs of God's promises. So let me remind you, since it can be so easy to forget in our country today, that every single member of the Republican Party and every person who votes Republican is a child of God. And every single member of the Democratic Party and every person who votes Democratic is a child of God. And so is every Independent voter, and every person who doesn't vote. All are children of God. And even more specifically, every member of the Trump family, without exception, is a child of God. And every member of the Clinton family, without exception, is a child of God. Maybe if we would remember that more often, we'd be less likely to dismiss and ridicule people who are different than we are.

In our polarized, divided world, Pentecost reminds of us that there is hope – the hope of listening, the hope of hearing, the hope of connection, the hope of communication, the hope of understanding. That is the Spirit that came upon the people in Jerusalem that day, and it is the same Spirit that is breathing and blowing in our midst today. Let's take another deep breath together now, and let's breathe in that Spirit of understanding. And carry that Spirit with you in the week ahead. It may be our only hope.

Amen.

III. Outside the Lectionary, Inside an Election

That Other Creation Story
Genesis 2:4b-25

June 6, 2016

If you've ever, carefully, read through the beginning of the Book of Genesis, you may have noticed that there appear to be two separate stories of the creation of the world – one of them in Genesis chapter one, and the other in Genesis, chapter two. The creation story in chapter one appears in the Revised Common lectionary, but chapter two, except for a few select verses, does not, and I actually think it is the more interesting creation story.

I hope you already noticed that the account in chapter two is quite different than the more familiar version in chapter one. I won't bore you with all the scholarly speculation about these two accounts of creation, one written by a source called "J," and the other by "P" and why they are there and if there really are two separate accounts or maybe the second is just detail about day six…but I think anyone reading these two chapters can recognize that there are differences between them. I hope you noticed, for one thing, the difference in tone between the very formal sounding: "on the first day God created the heavens and the earth" language of chapter one and the less formal sounding language of chapter two. The chapter one creation account is structured and ordered, each day something new being added to creation, in a logical, organized way. This chapter is fairly cold and mechanical in its narrative, almost as if it were written by an accountant or a physicist. But chapter two sounds very different.

I hope you noticed something else, too – in chapter one, human beings are created last, at the very end of the creation narrative, as if we humans are the very pinnacle of creation itself, what it has all been leading up to. And it is there at the end that God says we humans are made in God's image, and then God says: "Go and take dominion over creation," a phrase and a word, "dominion" that has been misinterpreted and used to defend a lot of awful behavior ever since. But in chapter two, humankind is created first, or at least near the front end of the process. There is dirt and there is water, and then God creates man, "*adam*," out of the mud, "*adamah*," by breathing into it the "breath of life." Unlike chapter one, which implies that we are the pinnacle of creation, made in the image of God, chapter two reminds us that we are made out of mud. John Calvin said about that particular aspect of Genesis chapter two: "if this does not teach us humility, we are more than dense." We are mud, dirt, dust.

Also notice that with human beings created first, everything else – plants, animals, the whole rest of creation – is created by God FOR us as a gift, to be enjoyed, not dominated. God makes trees so we can enjoy looking at them and eating their fruit and climbing them and putting tire swings on their branches. So it is with all of creation, it is a gift to be enjoyed, it is not for us to dominate and destroy. Creation is a gift, to be tended and cared for as you would any precious gift given by a special person you love and who loves you. Our very relationship to nature, and perhaps even to God, sounds so very different here than in chapter one. Chapter two is poetic, all about relationships: our Creator's relationship with Adam and with us and with all that God has made. Chapter two offers that great moment when God has created all the other animals and birds and then brings them before Adam and says: "What would you like to name them?" Another amazing gift – the gift for Adam to give every creature its name, its very identity. And Adam does: "Oh, that looks like a rhinoceros, and that's clearly a hippopotamus, and that's a platypus, and that, well, that's a slug" and these names become their identity. There is a relationship between Adam, and thus all human beings, and the other creatures with whom we share this planet. Then there's the relationship with God, which here in chapter two is not just God saying rather coldly, "go and take dominion over creation" but God expressing concern for Adam, God being afraid that Adam will be lonely. That's why God makes all the other animals and creatures and parades them before Adam to name. God's trying to find a companion, a helper, a partner, a friend for Adam. God really cares about Adam's well-being. So you might imagine God watching closely as each animal comes by and Adam names it, almost like speed-dating: "Hmmm, well, the hippopotamus seems nice, but he and Adam don't really seem to be bonding particularly well," so God finally says to Adam: "it is not good for you to be alone, so let's make a helper, a companion, a partner specifically for you, maybe with fewer horns and tusks and teeth than some of these other animals." And this companion will be made not out of the dirt this time but out of the very stuff that Adam is made from, his own living being, from Adam's rib. Someone to walk by Adam's side because she is made from Adam's side, literally. Or at least figuratively.

This is so much more interesting and intimate a story of creation than chapter one. All those scientific debates about creationism and evolution and Intelligent Design, they always focus on chapter one rather than chapter two, but it is this chapter that gives the personal, intimate portrait of creation full of life and relationships and poetry, the real stuff of life itself. It reminds me of one of the books in the Chronicles of Narnia, by C. S. Lewis, which have been favorites of mine since I was a child. They are great reading for all ages. My personal favorite of all the books in the series is the one that offers Lewis's account of the creation of Narnia, called The Magician's Nephew. Lewis picks up on the poetry of Genesis chapter two, as the animals are created and they are all kind of talking to each other and wondering "who are we, and why are we here?" and it is a wonderful scene, a fictionalized account that retains the tone and poetry for chapter two of Genesis.

This is not dry, cold, logical, organized pseudo-science, this is the poetry of relationships and mud and God getting God's hands dirty and chatting with Adam and worrying about Adam and then creating a woman to be with Adam, to accompany him on his journey. It is interesting that God puts Adam to sleep in order to create the woman, so there is no doubt about Eve's creation, it is not like Adam just wandered off into the bushes and found her, no he wakes up and sees her and says: "This is bone of my bone, flesh of my flesh." This is a love story, folks! There's none of Paul's later nonsense about woman keeping quiet or being subservient here – this is love at first sight, for Adam's equal partner, created by God, to enhance his life. But the love story is deeper and richer and broader than that – Chapter two is a love story between God and us and all of creation. And none of this is found in Genesis chapter one.

Oh, and just to give John Calvin his due, since he often gets a bad rap these days, Calvin said about the rib thing: "Thus Adam did lose a rib, but he was repaid for it with a far richer reward since he obtained a faithful and lifelong companion." You didn't know Calvin was a romantic, did you? That's what chapter two of Genesis does, even for a seemingly cold fish like John Calvin: it brings out the poet and the romantic.

I don't want us to miss how this passage ends. Adam and Eve are there in this garden, this paradise, everything you could want is there, as a gift from God to them and for them. Well, except for that one tree, but that's another story. And we are told that Adam and Eve are naked. Innocent. They had nothing and they had everything. And we are told they felt no shame. No regret. No guilt. They are just there with God and the hippopotamuses and the slugs and the trees and it is paradise. Heavenly, even. Love and relationship and joy. It's unfortunate that the story couldn't just stop there.

Amen.

Keeping Our Brothers and Sisters
Genesis 3:22 – 4:16, 25-26

June 19, 2016

I suppose it makes sense. I can hear those who put together the Revised Common Lectionary asking themselves if they really wanted to make preachers come up with sermons about Cain and Abel and deciding to just make preacher's lives a little easier by leaving it out. And yet I am also a little bit amazed that this story is not in the lectionary because it is the story of the first recorded murder in human history, a story of how bitterness and envy and jealousy and hatred can lead to violence. Which means this story is as relevant and contemporary as today's newspaper. It is fortunate that Cain only had access to a rock or else he might have wiped out the whole human race by the 4th chapter of Genesis.

I included the end of Genesis chapter three, which also does not appear in our lectionary, because it reminds us of why Adam and Eve are driven out and kept out of Eden. It is not really as a punishment, necessarily, it is because they have already disobeyed and eaten of the fruit of one of those trees, the Tree of the Knowledge of Good and Evil, and God realizes there is one more tree in that garden that they are not supposed to eat from and that is the Tree of Life. Or maybe they were allowed to eat from that one before, but not now. God says, "I don't want Adam and Eve, or any human being, eating from that tree or else they'll live forever." Again, maybe this is a change. Maybe God didn't mind them living forever in Paradise, in Eden, but now that they have disobeyed, and will suffer the consequences, God doesn't want them to have to suffer that way forever, in this "fallen" state in which we now live. So God wants to keep them away from that other tree, not run the risk of them having to live with the consequences of their disobedience forever. That's why God places the cherubim there with the flaming sword, to keep Adam and all human descendants of Adam away from eternal life in this world. It is not punishment, really – it is out of compassion and concern for us.

By the way, if you want to read a creative and powerful account of why eating from this Tree of Life would be a curse, I would again recommend to you <u>The Magician's Nephew</u>, one of the Chronicles of Narnia books by C. S. Lewis. Lewis offers a very interesting take on what a curse it would be to eat of the fruit of the Tree of Life.

Back to Genesis. Cain and Abel are the first children born to Adam and Eve and what is particularly interesting is that Cain and Abel might be twins. We are told that Adam "knew" his wife Eve and she gave birth to Cain and we're told immediately that she also gave birth to Abel, as if no time has passed. Regardless of whether they are indeed twins, we do know for sure that Cain is the firstborn, the older brother. This story sets the pattern that is found throughout the Book of Genesis of the younger brother usurping and supplanting the older brother. Think of Jacob and Esau, think of Joseph and all his older brothers, or less well-known perhaps are Joseph's sons Manasseh and Ephraim. In all these cases, at least in God's eyes, the younger is favored over the older. That starts here, right away, with the first two brothers in the Bible.

There may have been some tension between them from the beginning, as there often is with siblings, but Scripture makes clear there was tension between them in their adult life because of their respective professions. Cain follows in Adam's footsteps as a tiller of the ground, a farmer, whereas Abel is a sheep herder, a rancher, a shepherd. If you are a fan of classic Hollywood Westerns as I am, you will know that this is the eternal frontier tension between farmers and ranchers, there's even a song about it in the musical "Oklahoma!" – The Famer and the Cowman Should Be Friends. But they aren't, at least not here in the 4th chapter of Genesis. All of this leads to an act of worship; both Cain and Abel bring offerings to God. Cain brings some of the produce he has grown, and Abel brings, and we are specifically told this, the "first fruits" of his flock, the fattest and best portions. God is pleased by Abel's offering but not by Cain's. And here is one of the great mysteries of this story: Why is God pleased with one and not the other? Maybe God just prefers meat to vegetables. Many scholars have suggested that it is because of the intention behind the offering or the way it was offered to God. Again, Scripture says clearly that Abel offered the "first fruit," the best of his flock, whereas Cain simply brings an offering, we're not told whether he brought the first and the best of what he had grown. Abel brings the best, his heart is in it, and perhaps Cain is just going through the motions. Many of our ancestors in faith, at least in the Protestant Reformation, took this a step further and claimed that the difference was that Abel worshipped out of faith, whereas Cain was just doing what his father had done, just going to church because he was told to by his parents, in essence. The Protestant reformers said this should be a lesson to us that we are saved by faith, not by actions, not by works. Bringing an offering isn't enough if your heart isn't really in it.

Whatever the reason, God prefers Abel's offering. Now Cain was not too happy about this, and Scripture tells us his "countenance fell" - he pouts, he gets angry. "It isn't fair that God likes my brother's offering better than mine. Dad always did like him best." Cain gets jealous. Bitter. And his bitterness becomes hatred for his very own brother. And God comes to Cain and God asks him: "Why are you angry?" It's a great question.

It reminded me of the story of the Prodigal Son, also about two brothers, the youngest of whom goes off and squanders his inheritance and then when he returns home the father welcomes him and throws him a party. The older brother pouts, his "countenance falls," he gets angry and jealous and says to his father: "I'm not going into the house for a party. How dare you." And the father comes to him and asks the same question God asks Cain: "Why are you angry?"

I was also reminded of the parable of the workers in the vineyard. You remember that those who began working first thing in the morning, the "elder" workers if you will, with seniority, are promised a fair day's wage. At the end of the workday, the owner of the field calls the youngest workers, the ones who have only been there an hour, to his office first, ahead of the full day workers, and gives them a full day's wage. The workers who have been there all day start pouting, their "countenance falls," and they get angry and jealous: "We've been here the whole day. How dare you treat us this way." And the owner of the vineyard asks that question: "Why are you angry?" Cain – why are you angry? It's a good question for us to ask ourselves when we get angry and jealous and our countenance begins to fall: "Why am I angry?"

After asking this question, God then gives a profound warning to Cain. Notice that God doesn't dislike Cain, God has a relationship with him, God talks to him. Here God warns him: "Watch out! You can turn things around. Sure, I had some issues with your offering, but that doesn't mean you can't do better next time, if you don't let sin and anger and bitterness get in your way and become your master."

Obviously, Cain doesn't listen. He ignores this warning, and sin becomes his master. Cain gives into his anger and his bitterness and his jealousy; he goes out into the field with Abel, out onto his own turf, and Cain kills his brother. Then God shows up and asks him: "Cain, where is your brother?" And Cain answers a question with another question, one of the most important questions ever asked: "Am I my brother's keeper?"

A question we humans have been asking ourselves in some form or another ever since.

The answer is pretty clear, too. God doesn't come out and say it, but the implication is a resounding: "YES!"

"Am I my brother's keeper?"

"YES – that's the whole point!"

"Even Democrats?" "YES!"

"Republicans?" "YES!"

"Male, female, rich, poor, black, white, gay straight…am I my brother and my sister's keeper?"

"YES!"

Instead of hating them and being jealous of them and envying them, care for them. Keep them…safe, secure, fed, watered, loved, cared for.

Cain asks the question of God in a defensive way, clearly, but it is a great question for all of us to ask all the time, on behalf of every single person we encounter in daily life: am I this person's keeper? Yes.

Let me also mention the ironic aspect of this story, that the first murder grows out of an act of worship. Isn't that interesting, and maybe a bit chilling, also? Cain and Abel bring their offering to worship and that is what causes the bitterness, the anger, the pouting, the jealousy, the hatred, and ultimately the violence. A reminder that there are ill feelings even in church families…maybe especially in church families and around elements of faith. This story reminds us as well of all the violence that has been perpetrated over the centuries in the name of faith, in competition to prove oneself or one's group more worthy of God's favor than others. For that reminder alone, this story should be in the lectionary.

So God says to Cain "you are now cursed," not "I, God, curse you," but "you are now cursed," not a punishment, but a fact. The very ground which you used to till and grow food in, which you used to bring life out of, you have now stained with blood and put death back into. The ground will no longer produce for you. Could there be any worse curse for a farmer? And Cain protests: "This is too much! I can't bear it. When I go out into the world people will want to kill me for what I have done, for what I have become." But God says, "No, I will put a mark on you which will prevent this"—notice this mark of Cain is not put on Cain so much to protect him but to prevent any further killing. As if God has, after just one murder, already had enough killing. Unfortunately, it didn't work. Indeed Cain's own great-grandson, Lamech, will arrogantly rejoice after he kills another man. And so on and so on and so it goes, unfortunately.

The mark of Cain didn't work. At least it hasn't yet. We are still envious, bitter, jealous, hateful creatures who lash out with violence against our brothers and sisters. The story of Cain and Abel is really the story of us, today, still; of us continuing to insist that we are not each other's keepers, of us wondering why God blessed them and not me. But friends, if this sin in our nature is ever to be ended, it is going to have to start with you and with me, in every relationship we have with others, pledging that we are not going to be like Cain. Pledging to care for every brother and sister in this world as best we can. We may never erase this stain of Cain we bear, we humans, but we certainly never will if we don't start trying to, right now, in our own hearts and lives.

Amen.

Could We Find Ten?
Genesis 18:16-33; Ezekiel 16:48-50

July 3, 2016

The story of Sodom and Gomorrah does not appear in the Revised Common Lectionary. On the one hand, I can understand, as I can understand about the story of Cain and Abel, we considered a few weeks ago, why the creators of the lectionary wouldn't want to subject preachers to having to preach on this story even if only every three years. On the other hand, as with Cain and Abel, I must admit I was a bit startled when I realized that the story of Sodom and Gomorrah is totally absent from the lectionary. "Sodom and Gomorrah" and much that is associated with those names, rightly and wrongly, is part of our cultural consciousness, a cultural reference point even all these years later, and yet, if a preacher follows the lectionary religiously (and I suppose there really isn't any other way to follow it), you may never read the story or hear a sermon on it in the context of worship.

So, in an attempt to counter that absence, as indeed this entire series of sermons on passages that fall outside the lectionary is intended to do, for the next two weeks we will consider the story of Sodom and Gomorrah, this week from Abraham's perspective, with some help from Ezekiel, and next week from the perspective of Lot and his wife.

I begin with some a quick reminder of where this story falls in the narrative flow of the book of Genesis up to this point. In the early part of chapter eighteen, these "men" who are referred to in today's passage – they are more than men, they are messengers, indeed angels – appear out of the desert and Abraham welcomes them into his tent, offering them refreshment and hospitality, In response these men have declared to Abraham and Sarah that Sarah is going to become pregnant and deliver the son that she and Abraham have always wanted. This is an announcement that you may remember causes both Abraham and Sarah to laugh, because it sounds so ridiculous, and thus their son will be named "Isaac," a name derived from the Hebrew word for "laughter." Then the story immediately shifts to the less joyful announcement of the destruction of Sodom.

It is very telling that in the beginning of today's passage God is thinking out loud, we are privy to God's internal monologue for just a moment: "I wonder if I should tell Abraham my plans for Sodom and Gomorrah?" And then God decides: "Yes, I should tell Abraham. Abraham is the person I have chosen to be the father of a great nation; he deserves to know what I am planning to do." This is pretty extraordinary, don't you think? It is not often we are given a glimpse into God's thoughts like this, but it also reminds us that our God is not a God of secrets and deception. Our God is a God of revelation, not redaction. Our God is a God who wants us to know what God is doing, at least as best we can grasp it. Many times we miss God's signs and God's attempts to tell us what God is up to, or we can't truly comprehend them, but it is not because God doesn't, at least a times, try to let us know.

So God tells Abraham what is going to happen to Sodom and Gomorrah. Let's pause at this point to talk about the "sin" of Sodom and why it is going to be destroyed. This is where I'd like to bring in the passage from Ezekiel, but also to point out that there are other prophets – Isaiah, Zephaniah – who talk about the "sin of Sodom." Let's be clear what Scripture does NOT say about the sin of Sodom. The sin of Sodom was not about sex, it was not homosexuality. That's not even mentioned in Genesis or Ezekiel. Ezekiel states, clearly and plainly, that the sin of Sodom was "pride," arrogance, "prosperous ease." This was a city which was rich and prosperous, but they did not help the poor and the needy. The sin of Sodom is the sin of pride and of selfishness. The sin of being richly blessed and not being willing to share those blessings with others. Now that doesn't sound like any current culture or country, does it?

The pride and arrogance and lack of generosity of the people of Sodom is going to result in their destruction. When Abraham hears this, he tries to intervene, and this is where the story really gets fascinating. We're presented with an almost comic dialogue back and forth between God and Abraham.

Abraham says:" God, I know you are a just God, you will not destroy the righteous with the wicked, so if you find fifty righteous people, fifty people who are not proud, not selfish, who are generous, who are helping the less fortunate, if you find fifty such people, will you spare Sodom?"

God says: "OK, yes, if I can find fifty such people, I will spare Sodom."

Then Abraham says: "Well, what's five people more or less? What if you find forty-five?"

"Yes, if I find forty-five."

"Well what about forty?"

"Ah, sure, forty."

"How about thirty? How about twenty? How about ten?"

"Fine, "God says, "If I find ten righteous people, I will spare the entire city."

Now, like me, you might at this point wonder why Abraham didn't keep going. "What if you find five? What if you find one?" But the conversation stops at ten.

What I think is being presented here is how many good, righteous people it takes to change a society and to potentially spare it from God's judgment, from destruction. What is the critical mass of righteous people required to have an impact on a society? You get below ten, and what's being said is that it is going to be tough for them to do anything more than be saved as individuals. Fewer than ten people are going to find it difficult to make an impact. This is the reverse of that idea that most of us know about how a few bad apples can spoil the barrel. A few bad people can ruin things for everybody. I remember that Mr. Hutton, the principal of my junior high school, used to talk about the "five-percenters," the five percent of young people that behaved badly and messed things up for the rest of the class. This was forty years ago, so that number may be higher or lower now, if they were even accurate back then. Anyway in this story of Sodom we get the reverse of that – if a few wicked people can cause the destruction of society, can a few, or at least ten, good, righteous people save it from destruction? Clearly the message of this part of the story is "yes," if there are enough righteous people who are trying to follow God rather than follow along with the values of the culture, there is still hope. The culture, the society can still be changed. The city can be saved from itself. There need to be enough righteous people to make a difference beyond their own individual fate.

This is a message that should speak to all of us here in the modern world, in the culture in which we find ourselves, and perhaps make us ask some tough questions of this culture and the communities in which we live. Are we on the side of God's principles, of humility and generosity and taking care of those in need, especially of those in need? Or are we too often following the messages of our society and culture, the message that we're #1, that we should be looking out for ourselves first, that we only take care of you if we think you deserve it? The latter is Sodom thinking. The question is where do we fall, literally? And are there enough still trying to follow God's way and God's values?

These are interesting questions to be asking on this Fourth of July weekend. This weekend when we celebrate the principles that we lift up as a nation from our founding moment, are we still following them? Should we follow them? And I'm not trying to bring you down on this holiday weekend, but I think these questions are worth pondering: what do you, what do we, as Christians and/or as Americans, stand for? And are there enough of us willing to stand up for those things, to try to live them out as individuals and as a community of faith? Are there enough of us to make a difference, before it's too late?

Amen.

Don't Look Back
Genesis 19:1-3, 12-26; Luke 9:57-62

July 10, 2016

We pick up right where we left off last week, with Abraham having asked God whether, if he finds ten righteous people, God will spare the city of Sodom. As we shall see, God will find exactly one righteous person and the city will not be saved from destruction.

That one person is Lot.

Lot doesn't appear a lot (pun intended) in the readings in the Revised Common Lectionary. Many of the stories in Genesis involving him have ended up on the cutting room floor, so to speak. That's unfortunate, because I have always found Lot a very interesting, intriguing, figure in the narrative of Genesis. There's always something a little strange about every story in which Lot is involved. He first appears when Abraham is going to head off to the Promised Land of Canaan and his nephew Lot goes along with him. Literally, that's what Genesis says: "So Abram went up from Egypt…and Lot with him." Like a third wheel. And then the Bible says they are so successful, their herds get too large to be in the same place, and also the people taking care of their respective flocks start fighting with each other. So Abraham and Lot decide to separate, and Abraham says to Lot: "Hey, I will give you first dibs on the land," and Lot says: "OK, I'll take the best land, right over there in that fertile valley of the Jordan," which is where Sodom and Gomorrah are. This has always struck me as strange, because you'd think Lot as the younger man might have said: "Thank you, Uncle, but you deserve first pick." Instead Lot just takes the best piece of land for himself, with, as we read today, some rather unpleasant consequences, ultimately.

There's another story about Lot in Genesis, after he parts ways with Abraham, where he gets kidnapped and Abraham has to take a whole army of men with him and fight a battle to rescue him. At that point, again, I would expect Lot to apologize and maybe even say: "Hey, Uncle, now you really deserve to come and live on this land I chose; you've earned this fertile Jordan valley." But he doesn't. Maybe that's why this story of Lot's rescue ends by telling us that Abraham "brought back all the goods, and also brought back his nephew Lot." Almost as an afterthought.

Granted, Lot is a righteous person, he's the one righteous person found in Sodom, at least in comparison to everyone else who lived there. Yet I think you can hear a certain odd quality to this story about Lot as well. We find Lot just outside the city gates, waiting, like a one-man hospitality committee to welcome visitors. These men (OK, we know they are angels because we saw them before in the last chapter with Abraham), show up and Lot says: "Stay with me," and he even makes dinner for them. Lot is welcoming and hospitable and gracious, he is clearly his uncle's nephew. He is a good person, he has not fallen into the "sin" of Sodom, into pride and selfishness, as you may remember from last Sunday.

These angels now say to Lot: "We're about to destroy this place, so take your family"…in fact they really give him the opportunity to take anyone he wants, they don't specify who it has to be, it could be anyone else in Sodom…"and flee." And then we get this weird conversation between Lot and his sons-in-law, in which Lot is trying to tell them: "Hey, you've got to leave with me, this place is about to be destroyed," and I don't know if Lot was just not very assertive or persuasive, but they don't believe him. His sons-in-law laugh at him, they think he's joking. Lot's wife and his two daughters are the only people he can convince to flee with him.

I love the sense we get at this point that these angels are getting a little impatient with Lot. Lot hesitates, he lingers, he understandably doesn't want to leave his home and his city and everything he has built up over the years, and maybe even some of the other people he is leaving behind, because he knows it is all going to be gone. But the angels are saying: "C'mon, Lot, get a move on, you've got to get outta here!" It gets to the point where they are even tugging on him, pulling him, pushing him, "Go, get outta here!" And then they say: "Go all the way to the mountains." And then we get another strange interchange where Lot says: "I don't think I can make it all the way to the mountains, can't I just stay here in that little city over there?" And the angels are like: "OK, OK, gosh, you just can't help some people. OK, fine, you can stay there, just let us get to work!" That city, by the way, becomes known as Zoar, which in Hebrew means "trifle" because it is so tiny, hardly worth noticing. But as before, I wonder about Lot's behavior; instead of just saying: "Thanks for letting me live, I'll go wherever you want me to go," he's making deals here. It strikes me as odd. A little bizarre.

The story gets even more bizarre if you read on, but I'll let you do that on your own. Lot does become the father of two nations that will keep interacting with Israel, the Moabites and the Ammonites. But you have to read on to see how that happens. That is late night, R-rated reading, by the way. The Continuing Story of Lot: warning, not suitable for children.

Anyway, we get this other interesting detail here. The most familiar part of this entire story, probably. The angels give one last warning to Lot and his family as they are fleeing: "Don't look back." But Lot's wife looks back and is turned into a pillar of salt. And not to sound like a broken record here, but doesn't that seem a little strange, a little bizarre? In some ways it might make sense, this whole "pillar of salt" thing. This region where Sodom was located is roughly where the current Dead Sea is located, one of the saltiest bodies of water on earth. I've had the pleasure of visiting the Dead Sea, and you can see along the edge of that body of water not really pillars but formations of salt, so perhaps that's the reason that detail was added to the story, someone seeing one of these formations of salt and wondering if one of them was Lot's wife, or something like that.

Why would Lot and his wife and daughters be told: "Don't look back?" Isn't it interesting that Jesus, centuries later, gives the same advice in Luke's Gospel? Jesus encounters three people, potential disciples. The first one says: "I'll follow you anywhere," and Jesus says: "That sounds good, but let me remind you that foxes have their dens and birds of the sky have their nests, but the Son of Man has no place to lay his head." In other words, the Son of Man keeps moving and if you are going to follow him you've got to understand that this is a journey, you're not going to be able to settle down and get comfortable in any one place, we're going to keep moving, and serving, and doing ministry, with no place to lay our heads. Of course it is those of us who come after Jesus who have turned his religion into something settled, rooted in one place, with cathedrals and church buildings and Books of Order and creeds and such – but Jesus was about moving, you've got to keep going, there's work to be done, if not here than somewhere. Following Christ is a journey, not a destination.

A second person encounters Jesus, and Jesus says; "Follow me," and that person says: "Well, I will follow you but first I want to go bury my father who just died," and Jesus replies: "Let the dead bury the dead." In other words, you're alive, you've got work to do, your work is to go, spread the word of God's kingdom. Again a journey, work to be done. Life and ministry, and you've got to keep moving, don't look back.

Then Jesus encounters a third person to whom he says: "Follow me," and this person says "I'll follow you, but first let me go say goodbye to everyone at home" – not unlike, perhaps, what Lot was feeling when he delayed his departure from Sodom. And Jesus replies: "No one who puts his hand to the plow and looks back is fit for the kingdom of God." Now this may sound a bit harsh, rather like what happens to Lot's wife, but there is, I'd suggest, good reason for it. As followers of Christ on the journey of faith we are told: "Don't look back." And one reason may grow out of this image of the plow itself. I'll admit I have very limited experience with plows – I have used rototillers, and maybe it is similar – but I know you have to keep your focus on where you are going, at least I do when tilling, or else I suddenly realize I've plowed through half my yard and uprooted some bushes. So I think that is pretty good advice when plowing or tilling: put your hand to the plow and don't look back. You look back while plowing and you will turn in the direction you are looking, so much for a straight line, a straight row. Oops. It's tough to keep on the straight and narrow path if you keep looking back. This is also true of driving by the way, keep your eye on the road ahead of you, because your body tends to go in the direction you are looking. So don't look back if you want to stay on God's path, because otherwise you're going to veer off. Don't look back. Don't live in the past. Keep moving forward and keep looking ahead to what is coming, where you're headed, where you're going.

This is not to say we shouldn't revere and cherish the past or remember the past. "This do in remembrance of me." Just don't get stuck in the past. Remember the past, learn from the past, let the past guide you in avoiding the same mistake sin the present, but then let go of it, don't dwell on it, or in it. Because it is tough, if not impossible, to move forward while you are looking back.

This is true for churches as well as for individuals. The seven last words of a dying church are "we've never done it that way before." It is tough to move forward and change and grow if you keep looking back. God is all about the new – sing a new song, become a new creation, be open to new life, change, transformation. That is tough to do if you keep looking, or living, in the past. Gotta keep looking and moving forward.

That is the lesson of the story of Lot's wife: Don't hold onto the past. You know those past mistakes you've made? Let go of them – God already has. Don't keep holding onto them, move forward, keep going, keep looking ahead, keep on keeping on. Don't look back. Because God's kingdom is always about the new, about change and transformation and growth and life, and the Church isn't meant to be a museum, it is meant to be a living, breathing, acting, working, praying, worshiping entity. God wants us to grow and live, and if you keep looking back, you're just going to stand still…like a pillar of salt.

Amen.

Seeing the Face of God
Genesis 32:3-21, 33:1-11

July 30, 2016

Today's passage offers the often the forgotten part of the story of Jacob and Esau: the resolution of the lifelong struggle between these two warring twins.

After Jacob stole the birthright and the blessing of his father Isaac from Esau, he fled and lived with his Uncle Laban, his mother Rebecca's brother. (I would remind you that Rebecca was the one who came up with the plan to con Isaac out of his blessing – this sort of thing runs in the family, as we'll see). Jacob stays with his Uncle Laban, works with his herds, and falls in love with Laban's younger daughter, Rachel. Laban says to Jacob: "Work for me for seven years and I will give you Rachel's hand in marriage," and Jacob agrees, eagerly. Seven years pass, the wedding day arrives, the ceremony takes place, and when Jacob lifts the veil of his new bride, he finds it is not Rachel, but her older sister, Leah. Laban offers a rather lame excuse: "Well, marrying off the younger daughter first, we just don't do that around here." Jacob is still in love with Rachel, so Laban strikes a new deal with him: "Just give me seven more years of work and Rachel will be yours." Jacob agrees.

Later, Laban asks Jacob what sort of salary he wants for all the work he is doing. Wives are one thing, but let's take real reward, shall we? So Jacob now proposes a deal: "Give to me any animal that is speckled or black, and when any new animal is born to the flock, if it is speckled or black, let it belong to me; any animal that is white is yours." Laban says: "Sounds good," and immediately takes all the speckled animals from the flock and gives them to his sons. But Jacob has a few tricks up his sleeve as well. He discovers that when the animals are mating, if he puts a piece of a tree limb with some of the bark stripped off it in front of them as they mate, their offspring will be speckled. So whenever the stronger animals mate, Jacob places these striped sticks in front of them and the offspring, strong and vibrant, are speckled. When the weaker animals mate, no stick, and the weak offspring are black. Gradually Jacob's herd of speckled animals grows and gets stronger and heartier, while Laban's share of the flock gets weaker and smaller. Ah, family! Eventually Jacob hears rumblings from Laban's sons about this, and decides it is time to go.

Which brings us to the start of today's reading. Jacob is fleeing from Laban and heading right back into the fire, back to his brother Esau. For obvious reasons, Jacob is terrified. He knows, as do we, that despite the years that have passed, Esau is not one to forgive and forget. So he sends a messenger ahead to Esau, you know, to try to soften him up or at least feel him out, see is he can determine how he will be received by his older brother. He gets word back: "Esau is coming to meet you…oh, and by the way, he's bringing 400 men with him." I would imagine Jacob is thinking to himself: "Uh-oh, I might finally be in trouble. The magic may have worn off, I might finally be getting my comeuppance." To Jacob's credit at this moment, he prays. Beyond all the not-so-good stuff that Jacob does in Genesis, one thing always remains true about Jacob: he trusts God.

So Jacob prays to God, who has promised to always be with him, and promised many offspring and a long life. Jacob prays: "God, I trust in you. But I'm afraid of my brother, afraid of what is going to happen to me. You, God, have promised me all these things, and I trust you. Of course, I will also be trying to figure out whatever I can do to help my odds, here." This is, after all, Jacob. So he shrewdly divides his camps, and sends everyone on ahead, along with some groups of livestock as gifts for his brother. And Jacob stays behind and spends the night alone before crossing the river Jabbok.

I should point out that between our reading in chapter 32 and our reading in chapter 33 lies the great story of Jacob wrestling with an angel, with God, at Peniel. That piece of the story is in the Revised Common Lectionary, you've heard it before, and I have preached on it before.

So let's pick up Jacob in chapter 33, limping after that wrestling match, going out to meet his brother Esau. We've last seen Esau, some twenty years earlier: furious, spewing hatred and venom towards Jacob and vowing to kill him if he ever gets his hands on him. So it is again to Jacob's credit that he goes out in front of the women and children, bows seven times before his brother, and waits. That must have taken a fair amount of courage…and faith. Especially because Esau starts picking up speed and is soon sprinting towards him, as if on the attack. But instead, like the father in the story of the Prodigal Son, Esau opens his arms and embraces Jacob, kisses him and they both weep. At least one of them out of sheer relief.

Then Jacob says to his brother: "In you I see the face of God."

And, sure, he's a con man but I think he means it.

Now we see Esau's greatest moment in Genesis, and maybe a moment when he reverses a bit the curse of Cain, the bitterness of the older brother against the younger – he forgives his brother and Esau says: "You are my brother. I'm not sure I see the face of God in you…" Esau isn't willing to go quite that far. But he acknowledges: "You are my brother." And they reconcile. These two brothers who had been enemies come back together.

Now, I don't think these two became best pals or anything. The next thing that happens is they go their separate ways and at least according to Genesis they will not see each other again until the father Isaac's death, but they have reconciled.

It is an important and profound end to their story. This story very easily could have ended up the way the story of Cain and Abel did, with murder. But it doesn't. Maybe because there is some time, and distance, involved, in which heated emotions can cool a bit. Maybe because Esau and Jacob are able to rise above any feelings of bitterness or unfairness or hatred and recognize that they are both not only children of Isaac and Rebecca, but both children of God, as well.

All of which seems to me a pretty valuable lesson for us, too, in these times in which we live. Here in the summer of 2016 we are entering what I fear may be one of the most divisive election seasons ever. There seems to be rancor and division all over the place these days. Not just Democrat and Republican, but pick your various divisions: black vs. white, old vs. young, rich vs. poor, male vs. female, gay vs. straight, Arab vs. Jew, Sunni vs. Shia.

If Esau and Jacob can come back together…who would have predicted that? But somehow, they come back together, see each other, see themselves as brothers, see the face of God in each other: "we may not like each other, but we can't deny that we are kin – kin not just of earthly parents, but of our heavenly God." That gives me hope that maybe even Democrats and Republicans might be able to recognize themselves as brothers and sisters, fellow human beings. That maybe Israelis and Palestinians, rich and poor, black and white, all these divisions we are so good at creating, that maybe we all could learn a lesson here. I mean if big, dumb Esau can figure out that "I need to forgive this brother of mine," and if sneaky, clever, con man Jacob can have the humility and courage to say: "in you, brother, I recognize the face of God," maybe there's hope for us to recognize and do these things as well. I've got to hold on to that hope. And I invite you this week, these next 100 days or so until the election, to keep in mind Jacob and Esau. Because if these two can be humble and forgive each other and see each other as brothers and come back together, certainly we can. With God's help.

Amen.

On the Cusp of God's Promise
Numbers 13:25 – 14:45

August 21, 2016

This morning we read about an important moment in the history of the Hebrew people.

And we get a clear answer to a question that confuses many, which is "Why did God make the Israelites wander for forty years in the wilderness before they could enter the Promised Land?" This passage in Numbers gives us one answer. I would also suggest there may be a message about stewardship in this passage as well. We'll get to that.

First, this is a great story in and of itself. It is easy to forget that when the Israelites set off into the wilderness, God didn't intend for them to wander there long. They initially head to Mount Sinai where they receive the Ten Commandments, twice, after Moses destroys the first set of tablets in his anger about the Golden Calf, so he has to go back up and get another copy, which takes time. So they stay there at Mount Sinai for quite a while. They build the ark of the covenant, and a tent in which to house it, and then, after a year or so, they finally depart from Sinai towards the promised Land of Canaan. At this point, presumably, God is intending them to go straight there. So they go and camp across the Jordan from Canaan and Moses sends some spies into the land to check it out, to do some reconnaissance.

He sends twelve spies, one from each of the tribes of Israel. They stay in the Promised Land for forty days. They come back with big bunches of grapes, although when I was a kid, I always imagined them carrying bottles of milk and jars of honey. Anyway, they come back and initially they give a good report about this fertile, prosperous land they have seen. They also report there are people living there and some of their cities are fortified. And as they give their account, ten of the spies start to doubt, they start to wonder out loud if the Israelites will really be able to take possession of the land. They start to say: "Yes, it is a great, fertile land, but the people there are so big and powerful, they're like giants," and they compare them to a famous race of giants from Genesis 6, the Nephilim, who lived before the time of Noah. They claim they were like grasshoppers compared to these giant inhabitants of the land. "We don't think we're going to be able to take this land."

Against these ten, the two other spies, Joshua and Caleb, say: "Wait a minute, we can take this land, God has promised it to us. With God's help, we can certainly do it. With God on our side, what should we be afraid of? The only thing we have to fear is fear itself," or words to that effect. But as is often the case, the negative voices are louder and their pessimism begins to weave its way through the Israelite camp, and the people begin to grumble and complain: "Oh, why has the Lord brought us here? Just to get killed by giants? Oh, we should go back to Egypt, things were so wonderful there, remember how wonderful they were? Sure we were slaves, but we didn't have to worry about giants." The Israelites even begin having meetings for the purpose of choosing a new leader who will take them back to the good ol' days in Egypt. Make Egypt Great Again. It's such a human impulse – let's go back, back to what we know, even if it wasn't nearly as good as we remember. We're too afraid to go forward into uncertainty.

Moses and Aaron ask the people: "Why are you doing this?" And then even God comes down and asks: "What is it with you people? How many times do I have to send miraculous rescues before you trust me? The Red Sea parting wasn't enough? Manna, heavenly food outside your tent every morning, and flocks of quail that fly right into your camp when you complain about the monotony of manna, and water out of a rock – from a rock, mind you – when you were thirsty. Compared to all those miracles, helping you take control of the Promised Land is nothing. Why don't you believe me, why don't you trust me? What do I have to do?"

And that's when God decides: "I've had it with this generation. Anyone over the age of twenty who was part of your community when you left Egypt is going to die in the wilderness. Except for Joshua and Caleb."

Joshua and Caleb are the only two adults who were delivered out of slavery in Egypt who will also enter the Promised Land. And we are told why the Israelites had to wander forty years in the wilderness: God tells them they will wander in the wilderness one year for every day the spies were in the Promised Land. "Because you trusted the spies instead of me." God is telling the people that they are not ready for the Promised Land, but perhaps their children and descendants will be, perhaps future generations will learn the faith and trust their parents lack.

This is all about fear versus trust. The Israelites are so very human, like us. We who tend to grumble more than celebrate, we who tend to see the negative rather than the positive, we who tend to look backwards because that is not as scary as moving forward. And sometimes our problems, at least in our own eyes, can seem like giants to us in the moment. We see things from our limited perspective and forget about God's perspective. All of this really gets to the idea of stewardship, and not just because the Stewardship Committee asked me to preach a stewardship sermon today…

Stewardship is ultimately about trust and faith. I'm not just talking about stewardship in terms of money, either - money is certainly part of it, of course. When we as a congregation consider stewardship it is usually in the context of the reality that this congregation needs financial resources to carry on its mission and do its work. That kind of stewardship involves trust, pledging a certain amount of money, not knowing what the next year may bring financially. It is a pledge of faith, faith that God will provide, both to us as individuals and to us as a community of faith.

I don't want to sound like a TV preacher and send the message that if you give you will receive earthly prosperity in return. I can't promise you a new car or a better job or any of that, but I can tell you this, not just in terms of your money but also your talents and your skills and your gifts, if you are willing to put them in God's hands for God's use, even if this might give you pause because it sounds a little risky, you will be blessed. Because we are all blessed by trusting God and moving forward in faith. Blessed perhaps with a new attitude and a positive outlook; what the Israelites, except for Jacob and Caleb, lacked.

And so when the Christian Education committee approaches you and asks if you'd consider being a Sunday School teacher this year, and your first response is to say: "Well, I don't think I can do that, I don't think I'd be any good..." well, why not? What's the worst that can happen? I can assure you that any rumors of giants in our Sunday School classes are blown out of proportion.

So when you are approached by someone from the Session asking if you'd like to be on a committee, and your first response is to wonder if you'll have time or have the right skills, well what have you got to lose? What's the worst that can happen? I can assure you serving on a church committee will not be as bad as hundreds of years of slavery in Egypt.

Why not? Try it. God is right there, and if you fall flat on your face, God will pick you back up, I promise. And if God doesn't one of us will. Or vice versa.

Stewardship is about trusting and even risking a bit. Even when the obstacles may appear gigantic. "I'm going to trust that God will see me through and provide what I need to get the job done, to complete the tasks I'm called to do."

The tragedy of today's story is that the Israelites were right on the cusp of the Promised Land, right there, close enough they could literally taste it. And they could have gotten there forty years earlier. But because they were full of fear and didn't trust in the God who had already come through for them time and time again, they ended up in the wilderness instead. They weren't ready to receive God's promises.

Friends, I believe each one of us individually, and together as a community of faith and as a nation, indeed we as the entire human race, may always be living on the cusp of God's promises. Right there! We can see where we should go, we can glimpse the way forward, but we tend to get fearful, we give into our insecurities and our fears, we start blaming others and looking backwards, longing for where we once were. Instead I invite us to think about how we can be better stewards, knowing that we are living right on the border of God's promises, and that maybe all we need to do is be willing to take one step forward, together, in faith, trusting in the God who has always seen us through before. Because if we can't find the faith to do that as a congregation and as a country and as a world, we may never, ever, get out of this wilderness.

Amen.

Unexpected Allies
Joshua 2:1-24

August 28, 2016

It is unfortunate that the story of Rahab never appears in the Revised Common Lectionary because Rahab is a fascinating, and important, person in the history of Israel and of the Hebrew people.

But before I get to that, a reminder about the context of this story. This story may remind you of last week's story in Numbers when Moses sent spies into the Promised Land and ten of the those twelve spies gave a negative, scary report, offering the assessment that the land was too well fortified and the giants who lived there two powerful for the Israelites to take it. Two of those spies, Joshua and Caleb, disagree, saying: "No, with God on our side we can take it." The people side with the other ten spies, and because of this God tells them they will wander in the wilderness for forty years until all of them have died, and the next generations are ready to enter the land, with two exceptions, in that Joshua and Caleb will be allowed to enter the Promised Land.

So, we've jumped ahead those forty years now. Joshua is the leader of the people, the successor to Moses, who has died after being allowed to glimpse the land but prevented from entering it. And under Joshua's leadership, the Israelites are on the border of the Promised Land. Déjà vu all over again. Joshua sends two spies this time, not twelve, and he tells them to pay particular attention to Jericho, which was the first big city they would encounter lying close on the other side of the Jordan River, the crux, really for invading the whole area. If they are to take possession of the land, they will have to start with Jericho. So Joshua wants these two spies to scope it out.

The two men sneak into Jericho and end up at the house of Rahab. Why do they go to her house? All we are told about Rahab is that she is a prostitute. So these spies are supposed to be scoping out the city and they go right to the local brothel. I think I'll leave it to your imagination to consider why they might have gone there; we're never told in the story. But it doesn't seem the most logical place to start a reconnaissance mission; yet, maybe it was. Maybe a brothel was the Chamber of Commerce of its day, I don't know. Maybe they thought Rahab would know the people of Jericho, at least the men, pretty well, and she'd be a source of some potentially valuable information. OK, I'm willing to give the spies the benefit of the doubt and say that was the reason.

Regardless, it turns out they went to the right place, because Rahab has heard about the God of the Israelites and she is willing to help them. Which I guess goes to show that despite my skepticism about their motives for going there, God made sure they went to the right place to get help, as God usually does. Rahab agrees to hide them. You see, word has gotten around Jericho that there are spies in town, and the town leaders come to Rahab and say: "We hear that these spies came to your house," and, interestingly, Rahab responds: "Well of course they came here." Rahab is clever, and she knows how foolish it would be to deny that two men, after forty years wandering in the wilderness, might make a brothel their first stop while in town. Plus, her house is probably being watched closely, if not by her patrons, then by the perhaps disapproving neighbors. So Rahab says; "Of course they came here. But they didn't stay. I didn't know where they were from, I have my standards as you know, and so I sent them on their way."

Rahab probably realizes that the people--the good, upstanding citizens of Jericho—probably don't like her. I would imagine they may have looked down on her because of her profession, necessary as it might be. So she is ready to give her allegiance to the folks coming into the land to conquer it, especially if she can get on their good side from the start. Again, Rahab is clever, she knows what she is doing. She has navigated her way through life with intelligence and skill for a long time. So Rahab hides the spies, and when the people come looking for them, she says: "Yes, but they already left, and they went that-a-way," she gives them the old bait and switch, and points in the other direction. "If you hurry, you might just be able to catch them, too!" And off the townspeople go.

Now remember I already said Rahab is clever, so in addition to getting rid of the folks looking for the spies, she has hidden the spies on her roof, which means she has hidden them in plain sight. These are probably one-story homes, with flat roofs, and the walls of the city are taller than that, so from the walls of the city you can look out over all the rooftops. There is no way for the two spies to just sneak out the backdoor on their own, they need Rahab's help to get off that roof. Rahab has control over the situation. They can't escape without her help. Thus she possesses a strong hand and she makes a deal with them. This is the true art of the deal, folks. Rahab says to them: "I have already hidden you and I will help you escape, but in return, promise me that when you invade, you will protect me and my family." Of course the spies don't have a whole lot of choice here, and they try to hem and haw a bit, and make some conditions: "well, only if you keep our secret and only if you put this red chord in your window," as if they aren't going to remember which house is hers, which house was the brothel they came to first thing, but in the end Rahab gets her promise from them.

This incident always makes me think of the Passover described in Exodus, that moment when the Israelites put blood on the doorpost of their homes so that the angel of death will pass over, pass by, those houses, and the people in that house will be saved. Here it isn't blood, but a red chord that will alert the invading forces to pass by that house and spare the inhabitants.

Then Rahab says to the spies: "I have sent away the soldiers and the people looking for you and I will help you get out of town and when I do, go up into the hills for a few days, let the excitement calm down and you'll be safe." And she does, and they do. Rahab makes sure that, without her help, this whole mission, the whole invasion of the land, would not have been possible. Rahab is clever and she knows how to pick the winning side.

What's also interesting about Rahab as a figure in the Bible is that, although she is a woman and a prostitute, someone looked down upon in that society for a number of reasons, she is held up in the Bible as an example of a righteous, faithful person. Also worth noting is that she is a Gentile. Yet she is held up centuries later by the writer of the Letter to the Hebrews as one of the models of faith. This is in Hebrews chapter 11, a chapter all about the heroes of the faith, those people across history who have been faithful to God, and there's Rahab again. James, too, in his letter, holds her up as a model of righteousness because of her good deeds. And Rahab also appears in Matthew chapter 1, where Matthew presents his genealogy of the ancestors of Jesus. There's Rahab, along with just a few other women, part of the family tree of Jesus. This non-Jewish female prostitute is held up as a model, a hero, of faith and righteousness.

That may be the most profound message of this story of Rahab, this reminder that God can use, and will use, and does use, anyone. It doesn't matter what we may think of them, it doesn't matter what society may think of them, the fact is God loves to call people that the rest of us just write off, that we overlook or shun or ignore or label with derogatory names, those are the people that God always chooses and calls to do God's work. God loves to use people like that, partly, I think, to show us. And maybe also to remind us that none of us is as good as we might think, or any better than anyone else.

So I remind you of the story of Rahab, the story of the person who was really the crux of the entire invasion of the Promised Land by the Israelites. Rahab, this unexpected ally, chosen by God. Chosen not because of her position in society, but because she is smart and loyal and wise and faithful to a God, she really doesn't even yet know but somehow trusts already.

This week, as you are going about your daily life, especially if at moments you might feel underappreciated or overlooked, or as you encounter people that you tend to underappreciate or overlook, I invite you to keep Rahab in mind. To remember that good stewardship is allowing God to use whatever gifts we have been given by God, regardless of what anyone else may think, perhaps regardless of what we might think about our own gifts. Remember that the decision to use your gifts and your talents is really up to you, up to you recognizing that you might be the crucial cog, the cornerstone, in God's plan. Your opportunity will come. I invite you to remember Rahab, and to take it. God's entire plan might just depend on you.

Amen.

Lessons from Jericho
Joshua 6:1-27

September 4, 2016

This story of the battle of Jericho is one that I remember quite distinctly as a kid hearing in Sunday School. It is a great story, and along with it is this great song, which I also remember learning at an early age, "Joshua Fit the Battle of Jericho."

But let's acknowledge up front that this story, indeed the whole story of the conquest of Canaan, is also a little troubling, especially to our modern sensibilities. For the Israelites to take possession of the Promised Land they either have to displace the people who already live there or, as happens in today's story, kill them all. Why couldn't God have chosen a place where no one was living as the Promised Land, or simply given the inhabitants a chance to leave? I don't know. It would have made a more pleasant story than the one we have about the killing of everyone in Jericho except Rahab and her family.

I suppose there are at least two possibilities, one is that maybe the story has been embellished over the years, as human storytellers tend to do, the other is that God has some grand plan for good in mind that we have no clue about. Why did all the people of Jericho have to die, and the cattle and the sheep and the donkeys, too? I don't know. And perhaps this story hits a little too close to home for us as Americans, remembering how our ancestors came to this land of promise, and discovered there were people already living here that needed to, in their eyes, be displaced and even killed so we could take possession. So let's acknowledge that this story has troubling aspects to it and put that aside for the moment.

Because the story, despite those aspects, such a fascinating and important one, and one that resonates down to the present day. I am especially intrigued by the way the walls of Jericho come down. It is unfortunate that all the killing at the end of the story takes away from the fact that the city of Jericho is initially conquered without any weapons of war, without any swords or catapults or killing. The people simply march around and blow trumpets and shout and that's it. This is what we might call "psychological warfare." Imagine you are one of the residents of Jericho, and we know from last week's story about Rahab and the spies that the people of Jericho had heard about the Israelites. Their reputation precedes them. There is already some fear and concern about this conquering mob ready to invade their land. So imagine you are one of those people stationed on the walls of Jericho, ready to defend your city, and here come the Israelites on that first day, and you are expecting a battle charge or at least some arrows or something and all they do is walk around carrying an elaborate box on poles and blowing trumpets and then they leave, go back to their camp. Now even if you are a music lover, you might find this a bit strange, even troubling. What is going on? What sort of strategy is this? Then they come back the next day and you are ready for battle again, and the Israelites do exactly the same thing, they march around the camp blowing trumpets and then they leave, and I can almost imagine you might be pulling your hair out or at least scratching your head, trying to figure out "what are they doing?" I'm pretty sure some of the Israelites themselves might have been wondering the same thing by this point. And then they do it all again the third day. And the fourth. And the fifth. And by the sixth day you people of Jericho might have begun to wonder if the Israelites were going to do this forever, just march around your walls carrying their ark and playing music. And although it wasn't doing any damage, you might really be starting to stress out about this odd behavior.

Then on the seventh day those crazy Israelites start to do the exact same thing. This time, you know the drill, and expect them to leave after they circle the walls once. But they don't. The Israelites start to march around a second time. And then a third. And now you're really going out of your head: "Why the change? What's different about today?" After they march around your city seven times, they give a long, loud shout, a cry perhaps as fear-inducing as the infamous rebel yell from our own Civil War, and the walls.......... come tumblin' down.

Now I am sure there must have been over the centuries dissertations written about sound frequencies and vibrations that can somehow make solid stone walls crumble, how this shout might have physically caused the walls to fall, but that's not really the point. This moment is utterly miraculous and mysterious. Maybe even a bit ridiculous. Why would God choose this method for conquering Jericho? I don't know, but it worked. The walls came down. I think this gets us to the message of the story. It is not about battle techniques; it is a story about how God works. It sounds cliché I know, but true: God works in mysterious and miraculous ways. Especially when it comes to battles, and here I'm not just talking about conquering cities but the battles we each fight each and every day in our own lives. Whatever you may be battling in your own life right now, maybe you feel like you are waging some personal battles right now, maybe you feel like you are battling yourself, or battling others, or battling your own body with health issues or even perhaps battling God, and maybe these battles make you feel like you have run up against a wall, a fortress of some kind that you need to get around or through to get where you need to go.

Whatever battle or battles you may be facing in your life right now; I think there is a message here in this story for you. Think about some of the people marching with Joshua who must have been wondering: "What the heck is Joshua doing? What is God doing? Why are we wasting our time walking around blowing trumpets? When are we just going to take it, do what we came here to do? When is this battle going to be done? When is this wall going to come down?" This story is ultimately a story about trust. Trusting God, trusting that God is at work, even if we can't understand how. And being patient, giving God time to work out God's plans. If the Israelites had tried to take Jericho that first day, or the second, or any of the days before the seventh, presumably they would have failed. They had to wait. They had to march around those six days, perhaps wondering what God was doing, perhaps feeling absolutely foolish, too. Until the moment that God had chosen arrived, the right moment.

This is the message that Scripture reminds us of again and again: "Do not put your trust in the things of this world, in princes and horses and weapons of war, in armies or atomic bombs or Presidential candidates, or anyone or anything except God." Even if, especially if, you don't have a clue what God is doing or where God might be or why God is having you do something that seems incredibly foolish like march around a fortified city blowing a horn when that doesn't seem to address the real issue you are struggling with at all. The message of this story about the fall of Jericho is to wait, and to trust, and to know that God is working in your life and not to lose hope that eventually all those walls will come tumblin' down.

Amen.

God's Chosen
Isaiah 45:1-25

September 25, 2016

This morning I want to consider yet another person in the Bible who doesn't get preached about or mentioned in worship much because they never appear in the Revised Common Lectionary: King Cyrus of Persia. Cyrus is an unusual figure in the history of the Israelites.

You remember the Babylonian Exile, that time when the Babylonians invaded and took many of the Israelites back to Babylon. You may also remember that God had promised the people, most famously through the prophet Jeremiah, not only that this would happen but that it would only be temporary, if you can call seventy years "temporary," but God promised the Israelites that they would one day go back home. And the decades go by, and suddenly there arises this new king in Persia named Cyrus, also known as "Cyrus the Great." Cyrus begins to invade the territory of his neighbors, including Babylon, and he is wildly successful in these military campaigns. He invades Babylon in 539 BC, and when he invades, he frees those who are captives of the Babylonians, including the Israelites. Cyrus also allows those captives to return to their home countries. But not just to go back home; Cyrus gives the Israelites money out of his own treasury, as well as his permission, to rebuild their destroyed Temple in Jerusalem.

Now remember Cyrus is not Jewish. He's Persian. Yet God uses this Gentile king to bring God's people back home, and, by rebuilding the Temple, to bring God back home, too. That's really the message of the prophecy we read today from Isaiah – it is a reminder that God is in charge of all the events of our lives and our world, from the flap of a butterfly's wing to the rise and fall of nations, including the military success of Persian King Cyrus. It is particularly interesting that here in Isaiah we find words addressed to Cyrus himself. God tells Cyrus: "You are my chosen instrument. Even though you don't know me. Even though you don't even know I am working through you, using you as my chosen instrument." And probably Cyrus, if he ever heard these words of Isaiah, would have said: "Nonsense." He probably wouldn't have believed it. How could a God he doesn't know, or worship, be working through him, using him? Yet, God is, and does.

We are in an election season. In which, perhaps like me, at times you want to throw up your hands and say: "A pox on both your houses!" Who are these people we are going to have to choose between to be our leaders? Perhaps none of them are our first choice, or tenth or fifteenth or hundredth choice. So I find a certain ray of hope in this passage from Isaiah and in the story of King Cyrus, the reminder that God is in charge. And God can work through even imperfect and flawed leaders. Even leaders that you or I might think are awful and totally unfit. Which I'm sure some of the Israelites might have said about Cyrus. I suspect when they heard about his rising fortune and his military successes, they may have simply thought: "Here's another Gentile king, who cares?" I have to live in the hope that God is in charge, and that God knows what God is doing, even if we mess it up. That God can work even through bad leaders, somehow, and even they can serve God's ends.

Notice that this Persian King Cyrus is called the "anointed" of God. That word is used to refer to a number of historic Jewish kings, but in later times it was also come to be associated with the coming Messiah as well. Cyrus is anointed and used by God even though Cyrus has no clue about it. God declares: "This is the person I am going to use." Regardless of what we are going through in our lives, our communities, our country, our world, the ups and downs, all those times we hesitate to even open the newspaper or turn on the computer to read the news – yet another shooting, yet another natural or man-made disaster, yet another war, yet more violence, more darkness, yet more squabbling between candidates or people who support one candidate or another – yet the hope is that God is somehow working in and through all of this. Hopefully. Or else we're in even more trouble than we may think.

The promise of the prophecy of Isaiah is that God is at work in our world and in our lives, and that God has a plan. The problem is that we don't know God's plans. Oh sure, some people claim they do, of course, and sometimes we may think we see exactly where things are headed and what's going to happen. Or we wish God would just ask our advice about things, we'd set God straight on exactly what needs to happen. But the point is: God's in charge. God is a God of mysterious ways and unexpected choices. But part of God's promise is that God is working all things for good, ultimately. That's what I'm holding on to in these last weeks of a brutal Presidential campaign.

No one would have chosen or voted for Cyrus as God's instrument, especially not any of the Israelites, I imagine. Just like no one in their right minds, their human minds, would have chosen Jacob or Peter or Saul of Tarsus, but God did, because God has to, really, always work through imperfect, flawed human beings. And I imagine human beings don't always poll well in heaven, but God uses even us.

I find this passage a hopeful one for this election season we are in. I pray you will find some hope in it as well. For beyond all the uproar and the rigmarole and the polls and the slogans and the spin, God is in charge. God is working all things ultimately for good, often in mysterious ways, and I've got to keep believing that even if I don't have a clue about the how or the why or the who.

Amen.

Fire Escape
Daniel 3:1-30

October 23, 2016

I suspect there might be messages for us in this passage from Daniel that are relevant to this Presidential election season we are living through. The entire book of Daniel is about the conflict between church and state and in a wider sense the conflict between Divine authority and earthly authority.

The Book of Daniel has a lot of great stories in it, stories that we still reference in our culture even if the Revised Common Lectionary does not include them. In coming weeks we will read and consider the story of the writing on the wall, and the story of Daniel in the lion's den, but personally today's might be my favorite. Maybe just because of the names of the main characters: Shadrach, Meshach, and Abednego. I've always thought that would make a great name for a law firm.

As we jump into the story, a reminder that these three plus Daniel, all Israelites, have been plucked out of obscurity along with other young men to train them to be officials in the Babylonian King Nebuchadnezzar's court. Early on these four disobeyed the king by refusing to eat the official royal diet dictated to them, presumably a lot of rich food and wine, but certainly not aligning with the Jewish dietary laws dictated by God. Everyone else believes these four are just going to waste away to nothing, eating only vegetables and drinking water, and it turns out all four of them are stronger and healthier, "fatter" even the Bible says, than any of the other royal trainees who ate the palace diet.

In Chapter two of the Book of Daniel, Daniel interprets a dream for Nebuchadnezzar, so he is already making a name for himself. But Daniel himself does not figure into this story in Chapter three, only his three friends and fellow Hebrews Shadrach, Meshach, and Abednego.

It seems that Nebuchadnezzar, as do many people who are addicted to power and their own glory, decides to build this huge, gold statue of himself – ninety feet tall and nine feet wide - and then make sure everyone is commanded by law, whenever they hear the horn, flute, zither, lyre, harp, pipe, etc., to fall down and worship the golden statue. Which maybe reminds us that people who are powerful or desire to be powerful and their huge egos are nothing new. I mean building a gold statue of yourself, that would be like insisting you have to have your name emblazoned on every building or product you ever owned or something. At this point the story is almost ridiculous, not just the statue and the law forcing everyone to worship it, but even in the telling, with this list of musical instruments repeated over and over and over and the even longer list of the government officials the king sends for, the satraps and prefects and counselors and magistrates and such, it is almost like a Monty Python skit at this point. Laughable, really. Except for the fact that Nebuchadnezzar is deadly serious about forcing people to worship him at the foot of this statue.

Maybe you need a certain size ego to be a ruler or a king or a President, but I am reminded that the truly great leaders in history are often the reluctant leaders, whose true greatness comes from a certain humility. George Washington, for example, is perhaps best loved for giving up power, first as the General of the Continental Army and then as President, setting the precedent of not serving more than two terms even though he would likely have been able to keep that job as long as he wanted. Willingly giving up power is a rare, rare quality in a human leader. Well, Nebuchadnezzar displays no such humility or prudence. He wants everyone to fall down and worship him. And they do…except for three people. Except for Shadrach, Meshach, and Abednego.

There is clearly jealousy among the royal officials, and some of them who have been looking for an excuse to take down these three, come to King Nebuchadnezzar and say: "Hey, O Great and Wonderful King, remember those Jews that you brought into your court, well not only do they worship a God other than you, they refuse to bow down and worship your statue." So Nebuchadnezzar calls them in, and offers them one last chance to bow down and worship at his command, in fact he even taunts them, saying: "What god will be able to save you from me?"

We then hear from the mouths of Shadrach, Meshach, and Abednego, one of the greatest statements of faith in the entire Bible, a clear expression of what it means to have faith. They respond to Nebuchadnezzar by telling him: "We believe our God, the one, true God, can save us from you, and your fiery furnace. But even if God doesn't save us from you and your fiery furnace, we will still believe in our God, and not worship you."

That's worth repeating: "Even if God doesn't save us from you, Nebuchadnezzar, and the fire, we are still going to believe in our God." They are saying that their trust in God is unconditional, not based on what's happening or going to happen to them, not based on the circumstances of their lives, it goes deeper than that. It is not unlike what Jesus says about love, when he tells us to love our enemies or when he says that if we only love those who love us that is no credit to us, since everyone does that. Jesus says: "Love unconditionally. Don't love based on how people treat you, just love." That same idea applies to what Shadrach, Meshach, and Abednego are saying about their faith. They simply have faith, regardless of whether things are going well or not so well for them at any particular moment. "Even if we end up getting thrown into your furnace,

Nebuchadnezzar, we have faith that our God can save us from the fire, if God chooses to."

Regardless of what happens, no matter what happens to me in this life on any day, at any given moment, throughout the course of my entire life, I will still believe and trust in God. That's faith, friends. Pretty impressive faith. For most of us life seems pretty conditional. You scratch my back, and I'll scratch yours. I'll treat you well if you treat me well. Do unto others as they do unto you, which, by the way, is not the Golden Rule. When things are going well, we praise God. It is when things don't go the way we hope that faith gets tough, that praising God gets more difficult. When we don't see clear signs of God's presence and God's activity in our world or in our lives, that's when faith gets tough. So it can be tough to say: "It doesn't matter what happens in my life or how frightened I may be about the future and where things are headed, it doesn't matter how the election turns out, regardless of how anything in the future turns out, I'm going to trust that God is still here and working and in charge of things." That's faith. Especially when you are facing the open door of a blazing hot furnace, about to be thrown inside.

But that's what Shadrach, Meshach, and Abednego say. That is the faith they display.

And actually the rest of their story is almost anti-climactic after their statement of faith. Nebuchadnezzar, who is not just egotistical but thin-skinned and impulsive, too – not admirable traits in a leader – says: "Alright, I'm going to throw you in the furnace. In fact, I'm going to order it heated up seven times hotter than usual and then throw you in!" Shadrach, Meshach, and Abednego are bound and taken to the furnace, and the furnace is so hot that the soldiers who take them are themselves burned up on the way. And the door of the furnace is slammed shut. And then Nebuchadnezzar exclaims: "Wait a minute, instead of three bound men in the furnace, I see four unbound figures walking around inside, and one of them looks like a son of God," a divine being. So Nebuchadnezzar shouts: "Shadrach, Meshach, and Abednego, come out of that furnace!" And they come walking out, nonchalantly, I imagine, maybe whistling, just meandering, in no hurry, and we're told that not only are they unharmed, their bodies and their clothes are unsinged, with no sign of any fire damage whatsoever. In fact they look better, cleaner than they did before they went in, and we're told there is not even the slightest whiff of smoke about them. God has indeed delivered them.

And then Nebuchadnezzar, to put an almost ridiculous coda on the whole story, cries out: "From now on we must all worship the God of Shadrach, Meshach, and Abednego – in fact, anyone who disparages their God from this point on will be cut into pieces! And pay no attention to what I, Nebuchadnezzar was saying and doing just five minutes ago! Fake news!"

So it goes with earthly rulers.

It is a great story, and I believe it offers an important message to us: to put our ultimate trust and hope in God, not in any person or institution in this world. Ultimately, in terms of our faith, it really doesn't matter who gets elected or not, because our trust is not in any ruler or king or President. Our trust must be in God who promises to be with us every step of the journey and, ultimately, to save us. Even from bad kings. Maybe especially from bad kings.

And so in this fairly chaotic world and especially chaotic election season, when many people are on pins and needles, watching every poll, I invite you to take a deep breath and remember Shadrach, Meshach, and Abednego, and remember that we aren't to put too much trust in princes or powers of this world. Sure, it makes a difference, in the short-term, who wins elections, and we want good leaders rather than bad, if we can find them, but ultimately this story reminds us to put our faith, unconditionally, in the one Ruler and Redeemer who can truly save us, and who will never let us down.

Amen.

Writing on the Wall
Daniel 5:1-31

October 30, 2016

It is important for us as Christians, especially in this age of "fake news" and questionable information, to know what is in, and maybe more importantly what is not in, our Bible. I am always amazed when I hear people attributing certain quotes to the Bible. For example, the next time someone tries to tell you that the Bible says: "God helps those who help themselves," please reply: "No, actually that was Ben Franklin…and he stole it from English politician Algernon Sidney." Knowing the Bible is helpful, beyond the religious sense, because we still use many words and phrases in daily life that come from the Bible. I think it is important for us as educated human beings to know where these phrases come from and their context. In this morning's passage we find such a phrase, still fairly commonly used, which is "to see the writing on the wall."

We are at a period right now, both in terms of politics and sports, in which you might hear this phrase used in the week ahead. I am not going to mention specific instances, but it might be if your team is down by two games in the World Series, commentators might start remarking that they are seeing the writing on the wall, or if your candidate in an upcoming election is down 30 points a week before the election, you might begin hearing the pundits say they see the writing on the wall.

Now this phrase, "the writing on the wall," refers to what John Calvin called "an omen of calamity," a foreshadowing of what is likely going to happen, usually in a negative sense. That is what Belshazzar is given, a warning of what the future has in store for him.

What did Belshazzar do? Before I answer that it is worth noting that Scripture refers to Belshazzar as King Nebuchadnezzar's son, although many historians claim that he probably wasn't Nebuchadnezzar's son because history records another king in between Nebuchadnezzar and Belshazzar, so Belshazzar might be a grandson or just a descendant of Nebuchadnezzar. Nevertheless, Belshazzar has ascended to the throne of Babylon and as today's passage starts, he is throwing an elaborate party one night, a pretty wild party from the sound of it. Lots of wine is flowing, and Belshazzar is presumably drinking his fair share, if not his unfair share. And at some point, during the party, Belshazzar shouts out: "Hey guys, remember all those gold vessels and goblets in the treasury that were taken from the Temple in Jerusalem? Go get them, bring them to me, I don't want to have to wash these goblets we've been drinking out of, let's drink in style, all of us, including you, my lovely concubines." That idea is part of the sin of Belshazzar, to use these sacred objects, dedicated to God but now stolen from the destroyed Temple, for a profane purpose and by an obviously profane king. Wrapped up in this is the sin of idolatry, too, because, presumably just to add insult to injury, as Belshazzar and his party guests are drinking from these goblets dedicated to God, they are at the same time raising toasts to and praising their own pagan gods. Of course as Belshazzar is told later by Daniel, his gravest sin, a sin that most of us struggle against, is pride, thinking too highly of himself.

So in the midst of this party, as they are guzzling their wine from these formerly sacred gold goblets and singing praises to their pagan gods, a hand appears and writes a series of words on the wall. This must have been a pretty scary sight because it appears so suddenly out of nowhere, and the king turns pale white and even though he can't read the writing, his thoughts about what it might say and what this might mean, terrified him. I'm sure even Belshazzar realized this huge, ghostly hand probably wasn't writing: "Great job, Belshy! Keep up the good work!"

As the story continues, Belshazzar calls in all of his wise men and advisors and declares that anyone who can read the writing and interpret it will receive a purple robe and a gold chain and all sorts of power and glory, but none of them can. Probably because the words are written in Aramaic, which the Babylonians hadn't been teaching in their schools. That's one problem with not knowing other languages – if big ghostly hands appears and start writing on the wall, they might not write in your native language.

Then the Queen speaks up and says: "O King, remember that one Jew, named Daniel, who demonstrated enlightenment and wisdom and understanding way back in the days of your father, Nebuchadnezzar," or whatever relation they actually were, "remember how he was able to interpret dreams, try calling him. Maybe he can help."

At this point in the narrative of the Book of Daniel, it is worth noting that Daniel is probably well into his eighties by now. We often think of Daniel as young, but in this and the other great story about him, the lion's den, he is well advanced in years.

So Daniel is called in and he says to Belshazzar: "Keep all your gifts and your treasure and that purple robe, I will interpret this writing simply because God wants you to understand this message." That message being, in essence, a reminder that Belshazzar has not lived too well, that he is proud, that he commits idolatry, and that he has used God's sacred objects in profane ways. Because of these sins, those words on the wall: "MENE, MENE, TEKEL, PARSIN" offer a curse. These are financial words, they are literally about coins, but here they take on a more figurative meaning. The first word, MENE, means "to number or count," and so the message to Belshazzar is: "Your days are numbered, God is counting them, and they are running out." I'm reminded of the old joke about the aging baseball pitcher who asks God if there is baseball in heaven, and he gets the reply back: "I have good news and I have bad news. The good news is there's baseball in heaven. The bad news is you're pitching tomorrow."

The message to Belshazzar continues: "TEKEL: You have been weighed on the scales of God and found wanting, the scale comes up too light, out of balance." And finally, "because of you, the kingdom will be divided and given to the Medes and the Persians" which is Daniel's interpretation of PARSIN. This is a curse, a foreshadowing of bad things that are about to happen, and then the Bible says they indeed did start to happen, that very night.

All week I've been wondering how this story might apply to us in the current day, in this moment in which we find ourselves. We are at a moment in time as a country in which the division, PARSIN, seems particularly egregious. We are near the end of this election season in which we've got high emotion, with screaming and yelling and name-calling and negativity on all sides. And although many of us are looking forward to ten days from now when the actual Presidential election is over, I don't think that's going to solve the problem or lessen the divisions we see playing out. And so I wonder about this idea of "being weighed," the TEKEL part of the message. Is God weighing us as a nation? Being weighed in this story means being weighed on the scales of God, not earthly scales. On the earthly scale, Belshazzar appeared to have everything going for him – he was presumably healthy, he had been ruling for a while, he had more money that he knew what to do with, all the gold trinkets he could ever want, maybe even golden bathroom fixtures, so everything was going great for Belshazzar, according to most earthly standards. By that standard everything looked pretty rosy for the empire of Babylon, too. But to paraphrase what Paul writes in his First Letter to the Corinthians: "If you think you are standing firm, look out!" On God's scales, you may be coming up short.

I think this is, to some degree, true for all of us. We all come up short of what God wants for us, hopes for us, expects from us, that we are none of us ever as good as we may think we are or even as other people may tell us. God doesn't look at polls or voting blocs or bank accounts, God looks at the heart and the soul and the character, how we treat each other. "Love your neighbor as yourself," especially your neighbor who has a sign for a candidate you do not support in their front yard.

How are we doing on God's scales? This week I came across an interesting comment by one of our Protestant Reformer ancestors, Heinrich Bullinger, writing about this passage in Daniel. Bullinger writes: "You know we all," and I am paraphrasing wildly here, "we all come up short on God's scale because we all are too light until we have the weight of Christ's blood to save us and bring us into balance." We all are being weighed and perhaps found wanting, on our own. I wonder if our country is being weighed and found wanting according to the standards of God, of the heart and the soul and the treatment of others, especially the least among us? There is all this division and name-calling and bad treatment of people at the highest levels and trickling down. It seems like every day there is a new story about someone in a campaign saying something almost unbelievably rude and offensive to some other human being that they are running against, or their supporters. And the supporters of the candidates can sound even worse. I wonder about the tone of discourse in this country, even beyond politics, it seems to be trickling down into all areas of our national, communal life together.

"Love your neighbor, love your enemy." Treat everyone else the way you want to be treated, regardless of who they may be voting for or where they fall on the issues.

Are we being weighed as a country, and if so, are we coming up short, being found wanting? I fear so. I think today's story is a good one to keep in mind over these next ten days and beyond, and in doing so to ask ourselves: "How can we, as individuals and as a community of faith, help contribute to bringing our country back into better balance with God's hopes and God's expectations and God's scale of justice?"

I wonder if through this story God is reminding us that we'd all better read the writing on the wall, before it's too late.

Amen.

Praying at Open Windows
Daniel 6:1-28

November 6, 2016

As I have said in previous sermons, I believe there is an overarching theme in the Book of Daniel which has to do with the conflict between earthly authority and rules and God's authority and rules. Through that lens, today's story might remind you of the story of Shadrach, Meshach, and Abednego, in which they came into conflict with King Nebuchadnezzar who wanted them to bow down to the ninety-foot gold idol he had built. Today's story has a similar feel to it, the names have changed but the story sounds very much the same. Today we read about the conflict between Daniel and King Darius surrounding a certain decree Darius proclaims.

To give King Darius a little bit of credit, I suppose, unlike Nebuchadnezzar, who built that gold statue and his own inflated ego all on his own, this decree is someone else's idea, the idea of his other royal officials, who encourage him to pass this weird law that everyone must worship him for the next thirty days. A reminder that bad political advice is nothing new, it has been with us maybe since the beginning of time, but certainly since the time of Darius and his advisors.

Darius's advisors want him to issue this decree simply to undermine Daniel, because they know Daniel will not obey it and they are getting tired of Daniel showing them up by being such a good, trusted, honest, humble, God-fearing person. Bad people always hate that. So all the other, not-so-good advisors set him up through this decree which they convince Darius is a good idea. Darius probably likes the idea of everyone worshipping him for thirty days straight, and so he listens to them and issues the decree.

Daniel hears about it, and to me this gets us to the crux of the entire story. The centerpiece of this story is not really the Lion's Den, it is Daniel in his room after he hears about this decree. Daniel goes into his room to pray, as he does three times every day. And we are told an important detail about Daniel's room – it has windows which open towards Jerusalem. Daniel, remember, is one of the exiles in Babylon, so he prays towards Jerusalem, the former site of God's Temple, much as Muslims to this day still pray towards Mecca. I find those open windows a fascinating detail. Because Daniel knows he is going to be overheard praying. I'm no expert on 6th century B.C. Babylonian window technology, but let's just assume that Daniel is able to either open or close these windows. Did he always open the windows to pray towards Jerusalem, or does he deliberately open them now, after having heard this decree? Is he going out of his way to make sure others can hear him pray to a God other than Darius? Daniel is courageous either way, of course. If he always opens the windows to pray, then he is courageously choosing to keep doing what he always does, regardless of the decree. But if he goes out of his way to open the windows on this day, he is courageously showing that he especially wants people to hear him in the wake of this decree. Daniel's courage is either "I am going to keep doing what I always do," or "Especially now I want people to hear me pray." Regardless, this is an act of courageous faith. Daniel is choosing to disobey a corrupt law based on his belief, and he is willing to suffer the consequences. This is an act of civil disobedience.

I was doing some research for today's sermon and I came across a piece of information that I had not been aware of before. Mahatma Gandhi supposedly revered Daniel. He called Daniel one of the "greatest passive resistors who ever lived." Daniel is there in his room praying with the windows wide open, defying the law. Quietly and prayerfully, but clearly and powerfully. Gandhi saw Daniel as a great model of passive resistance.

To me Daniel praying at the open windows is the most important part of this story. The rest of it is dramatic, sure, but pretty much what you'd expect. Daniel is overheard by the sleazy conspirators who I'll just bet were waiting underneath the window in the bushes, and they go and inform King Darius, who feels bad about it but doesn't want to lose face by making an exception to his decree – Pontius Pilate, eat your heart out – and so Daniel is thrown into the Lion's Den and God saves him.

That moment of Daniel openly praying in his room gets us back to the theme about the conflict between earthly authority and Divine authority. History, and present-day life, are full of moments when earthly laws and God's law come into conflict, as they do here for Daniel. When faced with this conflict, the message offered in Daniel chapter six is: Follow God. And be willing, perhaps, to suffer the consequences of that decision.

I came across another interesting quote this week while pondering all this, a quote from John Calvin commenting on this story in Daniel. It is easy for us in the modern day to poke fun at Calvin, this somber looking guy with a funny, pointy beard, who probably wasn't much fun at parties, he certainly was not the party animal that Martin Luther was reputed to be, that's for sure. But we sometimes forget how much courage it took at that time to do what Martin Luther and John Calvin and others did, to take on a hugely powerful earthly institution like the Roman Catholic Church of that time, to believe so strongly that God was calling them to do something for which they knew they might severe consequences, even death. So here's a quote from John Calvin about this story of Daniel; I'm not going to suggest if or how it might apply to the current state of things in our country, but maybe it does. Calvin wrote: *"For earthly princes abdicate their power when they rise up against God*

— worse, they are unworthy to be accounted in the number of men. We ought rather to spit in their faces than obey them when they are so shameless as to want even to despoil God of his right and as it were occupying his throne." I suspect Calvin is speaking slightly figuratively about spitting in the face of an earthly prince, but the idea expressed is profound and bold and courageous.

Daniel was essentially spitting in the face of Darius when he chose to pray in his room with the windows wide open for all to hear.

I'm not sure exactly what this story might be telling us here in this concluding week of a divisive and combative Presidential election, but I suggest this: there's going to be a lot of sturm und drang in the coming week, regardless of the final result. It might be a good week to keep in mind this picture of Daniel there on his knees in his room, praying to the one, true God with the windows wide open, for all to hear, certain that God, not any earthly prince, is in charge.

Amen.

A Whale of a Story
Jonah 1:1-17, 2:1-10

November 13, 2016

Parts of the story of Jonah appear in the regular three-year cycle of the Revised Common Lectionary, but the portions we read this morning do not. I have preached on Jonah before, and you may have heard sermons about Jonah, but these early parts of the story of Jonah, the most interesting and familiar parts, including Jonah's motivation and the moment he is swallowed by that big fish, do not appear in the lectionary, so I am concluding my series of sermons on passages that do not appear in the lectionary with them.

It could be that some of you this week, given all that's been going on, including the Presidential election, have felt like you might, or all of us might, be living in the belly of a whale. Or maybe you wish you were instead of being subjected to all the news of the week; I don't know.

So let's jump in, shall we? Pun intended. Jonah is in many ways unique among the prophets in the Old Testament; I also think there are some intriguing similarities between today's story and the stories we have been reading in past weeks from the Book of Daniel and the theme of the conflict between earthly authority and Divine authority, which gets a slightly different spin – sorry, bad word for this week, let's say "english" – here in Jonah, but I'll come back to that.

When God calls someone in the Bible, it's very common for that person to want to resist that call, as we see with Moses and Isaiah and Jeremiah and others who respond with humility: "Who am I?" or even "Woe is me." But in all these cases the person called actually goes and does what God is calling them to do. What's unique about Jonah is that when God calls him and says: "Get up, go to Nineveh," Jonah gets up and goes in the opposite direction. He doesn't just protest, he runs away. Many other people in the Bible want to do just that, but they don't. To my knowledge Jonah is the only prophet who so willfully and deliberately disobeys and just runs away from God. This makes him so wonderfully human; don't you think? God is often tapping on our shoulders, trying to call us to some task or ministry, and I think many of us don't just resist God, we try to run away, sometimes in the opposite direction. I went to seminary with many people who had similar stories, of feeling God nudging them in the direction of ordained ministry, and some of them for decades did everything but go to seminary, as if they could wait God out – if I ignore God long enough, and focus my energy on another career, maybe God will just let it drop. But God never does. Trying to run away from God, although very human, is a ridiculous idea. Impossible. Where do we think we can go? As Psalm 139 reminds us: "Where can I go from your Spirit? Where can I flee from your presence? If I go up to the heavens, you are there; if I make my bed in the depths, you are there." But Jonah tries his best to run away from God, and God's call.

So Jonah is feeling this conflict, similar to the conflict we've seen in the Book of Daniel – the conflict between what people want and what God wants. Jonah's conflict, at this point, is on a very personal level – not what an earthly king wants, but what Jonah, himself wants…or thinks he wants. He is putting himself in conflict with God's will…for a little while, at least.

Of course as we see it is not just Jonah who is affected by his disobedience. His conflict with God pulls into its wake all those people on the ship with him, that ship sailing away from Nineveh. So as they are sailing a storm comes up, a storm that God is using to try to get Jonah to turn around, but it affects everyone on that ship. The sailors are trying to do everything they know how to do to save the ship, throwing cargo overboard and even casting lots and wondering: "Who is this Jonah guy sleeping down below? We think this may be his fault." I love that little detail about Jonah sleeping during the storm, it reminds me of Jesus sleeping in the boat during that storm on the Sea of Galilee. And it will, oddly, be Jonah who, like Jesus, calms the storm, but in a very different way than Jesus. The fact that, although Jonah is running from God, he is somehow able to sleep during this storm always astounds me, which is maybe more a reflection of my sleeping patterns than Jonah's. To his credit, when Jonah wakes up, he admits to the sailors that all of this is probably his fault.

And he tells them to throw him into the sea, and that should make everything OK again.

Notice that the sailors initially don't want to do that, they don't want to sacrifice Jonah, or anyone, to the sea. But they eventually run out of other options, nothing else is working, so they do. Into the sea he goes, and the minute Jonah sinks beneath the roiling surface of the waves, everything calms down, the storm immediately ceases. And then the story really gets interesting.

For one thing, we are told that the sailors have been converted by this incident, or at least their faith has been deepened. They worship God and offer a bunch of promises, probably having to do with becoming priests or giving up drinking if they ever reach dry land, that sort of thing. So Jonah has done a little bit of good already.

But what about Jonah? Although he has been thrown into a raging sea without much hope of survival, this is not the end of Jonah's story, not by a long shot. As if to add insult to injury, Jonah gets swallowed by a big fish, a whale. And as awful as being in the middle of the sea all alone might be, the belly of a whale is probably even worse, probably not the most pleasant place to spend any amount of time, especially not three days and three nights: dark and claustrophobic and warm and sticky and smelly and just disgusting. On the surface it would appear to be added punishment for Jonah. If someone was told they would be swallowed by a whale and spend three days in the belly of that whale, I think most people would wonder: "What did I do to deserve this?"

So it always strikes me as amazing that, in the belly of that whale, Jonah prays. And not a prayer of contrition and confession as we might expect: "Boy, God, did I mess up by trying to run away from you…forgive me." That's not what we hear from Jonah. Jonah instead offers a prayer of thanksgiving to God who he says has "already delivered me." "I cried out to the Lord in my distress, and he answered me." Past tense. Jonah is still in that dark, smelly belly of the whale but he is already praying a prayer of thanks to God for saving him and delivering him. As if what looks to be punishment might actually be salvation.

Remember Shadrach, Meshach, and Abednego in the Book of Daniel praying a prayer of thanks to God regardless of whether they would be delivered from the fiery furnace or not. They didn't see the furnace as punishment, but as salvation: "We will be saved, even in the midst of the flames."

Remember Daniel praying similarly about the lion's den. What looks like punishment is actually, with the eyes of faith, the means of salvation.

Remember the over-arching symbol of our Christian faith, the cross. It was a device used for torture, for punishment. But through Jesus, it becomes the means of our salvation.

God has a way of doing that. Just when things look dark and hopeless and impossible, and just when the situations we find ourselves in look hopeless, that we have no chance of getting out of this one, of being rescued, that's when we may discover that what we thought was punishment is actually a form of salvation, the vehicle, the vessel, through which God comes through yet again.

It is the whale and being swallowed by the whale that saves Jonah from drowning, and where he learns again that lesson. And it is the whale that delivers him safely, in a fairly disgusting way, back up on land. So as Jonah finds himself sitting there in a pile of whale vomit, he realizes he is saved. And, eventually, through him, Nineveh as well.

Yet another reminder of how God operates, and that God's ways are not our ways, and that when it looks dark to us and we begin to despair, when we can't see any light at the end of the tunnel, or the fish belly, and we can't imagine any way out, that's when God reminds us that what may have looked like Divine punishment was really the only way to turn us around and save us, to get us back on track, on God's path.

This is the so-called "sign of Jonah" that Jesus himself mentions in comparison to himself and his mission. The sign of Jonah, the sign of disobedient prophet offering thanks for three days and three nights for a result he hasn't yet experienced; the sign of unimaginable, unexpected, seemingly impossible deliverance even from within the dark, stinking belly of a whale.

Amen.

www.ingramcontent.com/pod-product-compliance
Lightning Source LLC
Chambersburg PA
CBHW052149110526
44591CB00012B/1907